Keeping a Princess Heart

In a Not-So-Fairy-Tale World

A CONVERSATION GUIDE for WOMEN

Also by

NICOLE JOHNSON

Fresh Brewed Life
Fresh Brewed Life Study guide

TRILOGY ON FAITH, HOPE, AND LOVE
Raising the Sail
Stepping into the Ring
Dropping Your Rock

NICOLE JOHNSON LIVE (VIDEOS)
Funny Stuff Women Can Relate To
Stepping into the Ring

www.princessheart.com
www.wpublishinggroup.com

Keeping a Princess Heart

In a Not-So-Fairy-Tale World

A CONVERSATION GUIDE
for WOMEN

NICOLE JOHNSON

W PUBLISHING GROUP
A Division of Thomas Nelson Publishers
Since 1798

www.wpublishinggroup.com

Keeping a Princess Heart
In a Not-So-Fairy-Tale World
A Conversation Guide for Women
by Nicole Johnson

Published by W Publishing Group,
a Division of Thomas Nelson, Inc.,
P.O. Box 141000, Nashville, Tennessee 37214.

Unless otherwise noted, all quoted materials are from *Keeping a Princess Heart* by Nicole Johnson (Nashville: W Publishing Group, 2003).

Unless otherwise noted, Scripture quotations are from the *Holy Bible, New Century Version*. Copyright © 1987, 1988, 1991 by Word Publishing, a Division of Thomas Nelson, Inc. Used by permission. All rights reserved.

Scriptures marked NKJV are from the *New King James Version*. Copyright © 1991, 1982, 1982, 1985, 1990 by Thomas Nelson, Inc. Used by permission.

Scriptures marked KJV are from the *King James Version* of the Bible.

ISBN 0-8499-4495-3

Printed in the United Stated of America

04 05 06 07 VG 5 4 3 2 1

For My Friends . . .

For all the meaningful conversations, day and night.

For the exchange of ideas that constantly shapes our thinking and changes our hearts.

These conversations have animated my thoughts and inspired this work.

YOU KNOW WHO YOU ARE.

CONTENTS

With Gratitude

I would like to gratefully acknowledge the W Publishing Group, David Riley & Associates, and Amy Cella for their hard work in publishing and designing this guide. Debbie, Mary, Patty, Corrie, and Toni—you've made this into a book that is so much more than just "talk."

A Note from Nicole

WELCOME TO THE CONVERSATION GUIDE OF *Keeping a Princess Heart*. We've designed this eight-lesson interactive guide especially for women who want to understand what became of their fairy-tale dreams, wonder, and joy. This guide is for women who work all day, in the home or out, who are desperately trying to make sense of what's going on in the world around them, as well as in the interior world within them. In short, it's for every women who would like to keep a soft, tender heart in the midst of a very hard and demanding world. If you're a little bit like me, you want to talk about some of these issues and not just read about someone else's experience. You want to listen to those you know share and talk about their situations as you process your own. This study will help you do exactly that.

The older we get, the harder it is to live with hope in the midst of difficult realities. We either hold on to false idealism or give our hearts over to hard cynicism. *Keeping a Princess Heart* is about finding the road in between.

I invite you to sit down with me and discover how you can find new joy as you revive your princess heart. I pray this study will be a meaningful experience for you as you venture with me into your own wonderful story and encounter the truest Prince of all times.

You may choose to meditate on each lesson alone in the privacy of your bedroom, or you may prefer to invite a few close friends or neighbors over to join you in your living room. You'll find this resource to be an invaluable tool for reaching out to the hearts of women by communicating hope and encouragement. As you begin to discuss common issues, you'll see that it changes everything for a woman when she realizes she's not alone in her struggles. And you'll find that as you recover your princess heart, there is a happily-ever-after ending for you with the Prince of Peace.

Let's Get Started

This Conversation Guide is designed for use by groups of varying sizes and with different-length sessions. It's also designed for individuals to use on their own. Because of these options, we have intentionally provided more material than you may need in your particular group. The advantage is that you can choose the parts of the material that are most beneficial for your members, or for yourself. Don't worry about not covering every single question in each lesson. Like any great conversation between friends, pursue the topics that peak your interest and lead to more in-depth discussions.

WHAT YOU'LL NEED

For this study, you will need a Bible, a notebook or journal, and a copy of *Keeping a Princess Heart*, along with its accompanying DVD. Before you begin, find what you'll need for each lesson in AT A GLANCE! And as a quick reference, in the back of this book is a list of all the AT A GLANCE sections, books to read, and movies to watch suggested for each week.

WHAT YOU'LL FIND

You'll find each lesson is divided into the following sections:

IN PREPARATION

Get the most from each discussion by being well prepared! This section will tell you which companion chapter to read in advance from the *Keeping a Princess Heart* book. It might also suggest watching a related sketch on the bonus *Keeping a Princess Heart* DVD, reading a passage from another book, or viewing a fairy-tale movie that connects with the lesson.

If you're meeting in an extended retreat-type setting, you may be able to show these movies and sketches to your group. But if your meeting time is limited, I suggest that the members in your group view these individually in advance.

LET'S TALK ABOUT IT . . .

This section provides thought-provoking conversation starters that you and your small group can really get your minds and hearts into. If your meeting time is short, look over the questions in advance and choose which ones you most want to discuss or will best fit your group's personality. Choose someone to be the group facilitator so that the conversation keeps moving. Make it clear that this person is not the "teacher," but rather a leader who will keep the discussion from going into Never-Never Land. You might even decide to rotate leaders for each lesson.

Encourage your group to agree that what's said in the Princess group stays with the Princess group. Once women feel comfortable and safe with your group, they will more likely open up and share their feelings. Watch for anyone whose pain is particularly deep and serious. You might need to refer her to your pastor or church counselor for further help.

DIRECTIONS TO THE INVISIBLE KINGDOM
In this section, helpful lesson-related Scripture will guide you to discover real-world answers to life's many difficult questions. Filter out the false messages by seeing the truth through the looking glass of God's invisible kingdom!

MIRROR, MIRROR ON THE WALL
This section allows you to face yourself as you reflect on some practical personal questions.

WRITE YOUR HEART OUT
Examine your heart and record your own story! Each lesson gives you guidelines for writing your thoughts in a journal or notebook. At the end of each chapter, you'll also be allowed to crystallize your thoughts and express how you feel about what you've just learned and choose how it has impacted your thinking.

DOES THE SHOE FIT?
In this section, I'll help you try the lesson on for size by asking you a personal question that offers a practical, real-world application.

PICTURE A PRINCESS HEART
Each lesson provides a list of theme-related movies, books, and CDs you might watch, read, and listen to which will expand your learning experience. There's even a space on that page to add your own favorites to each list.

PRAYER OF A PRINCESS HEART
Take time in this section to talk to God about what you've learned. Let prayer carry your deepest wishes, dreams, fears, and longings to the Prince of Glory himself.

Bridegroom

From the moment I first saw you,
I could tell that you were prized,
And even though you could not see it,
You are a princess in His eyes.
By the hands of the Father, the King of all eternity,
You were carefully created—to be—can't you see?

From the moment He first saw you,
He found in you His treasured bride.
Though at first you could not see it,
You are a princess in His eyes.
By the hands of the Father, the King of all eternity,
You were carefully created—to be—can't you see?

Jesus has waited all of your life;
He has waited long for you to realize . . .

You are a princess in His ballroom—
You are dancing, you are smiling and laughing—
Carried on the arm of the love of your life!
Oh, how He loves you and adores you—
And His joy in you is written all over His Face.
He is your Bridegroom . . . forever.[1]

WORDS AND MUSIC BY
CHRISTA SHORE

Prologue

ALLIE RANDALL FELL FAST ASLEEP WITH HER TIARA SLIGHTLY CROOKED AND JUST A LITTLE BIT TANGLED IN HER BLOND HAIR. *It had been a very busy day for the princess. Riding her bike to strange new lands, negotiating a peace treaty with the neighbors' dog, reclaiming palace treasures that lay hidden and nearly forgotten in the tall grass, and even being an ambassador of goodwill to her brother (not a prince), Nathan.*

After all, there was a lot of catching up to do.

It had been barely a week since her father had placed the little tiara on her head.

"It's beautiful," she had whispered in awe as he pulled it from his black suitcase that lay open on the bed. "Is it real?" She was kind of out of breath and scared to ask.

"Of course," her daddy whispered back close to her cheek as he gave her a quick kiss. "It belonged to a princess in Seattle, where I had to go for business this week." He turned the glorious little crown this way and that, angling it just right to catch the light, making it sparkle. Callie was in a happy trance under its dazzling spell.

Her mother smiled in the doorway.

Her father dropped to one knee, cleared his throat, and said in his most serious voice, "Callie," he took his time with each word, "you are a princess."

Then he did the funniest thing. He went to his briefcase and pulled a piece of paper from the many that were sticking out all over, and he rolled it up and put it to his mouth. "Doot-doot-doo!" he trumpeted. "Announcing, Princess Callie!" And he placed the tiny, glittering tiara very carefully on her head.

Callie stood straight up on her tiptoes to receive the crown. Every muscle in her little body was stretched taut as she walked slowly around the room, afraid her crown might fall off. Her six-year-old posture was perfect, and her tiny neck felt a full two inches longer carrying its precious cargo. Her arms were stiff as rods by her side, and for no real reason, her pinkie fingers stuck straight out. "I'm a princess," she said out loud and managed a twirl and a half on the hardwood floor. "I'm a princess," she giggled, "a princess in my pajamas!"

For six days the princess and her tiara had seldom parted. And behind the soft green eyes now closed in slumber, Callie Randall dreamed of castles, princes, and horse-drawn carriages. Meanwhile, in the bedroom next door, burgundy loafer heels clicked on the hardwood floor as Callie Randall's daddy packed his black suitcase for the last time.

She awoke with a start. Her heart was racing. Her hair was stuck with sweat around her neck. The cotton T-shirt she'd worn to bed was twisted halfway around her body, and her stomach was bare and cold. She stared hard into the blackness of the hotel room, trying to remember where she was. Room 6-something, but what city? Oh yeah, Atlanta. Franklin Howard Company. That was why she was here, consulting.

Awful day. Two glasses of Cabernet before bed hadn't made it any better, and now she had a thick, dry tongue and a slight headache. Her bladder was full, but she didn't move. The air conditioner cycled on, and a door somewhere down the hall clicked loudly. She wondered what time it was but didn't turn her head toward the clock. Her eyes were boring a hole in the darkness. I must have had a bad dream. Her heartbeat was slowing back down, and the sweat was making her cold on the back of her neck. She blinked. Her eyelids were dry. She needed to go to the bathroom, and she wanted to check the time. She did neither.

The words of an old song that Paul Simon sang washed over her. "A good day ain't got no rain . . . A bad day is when I lie in bed and think of things that might have been." The tender prick of a tear stung her eye. She felt paralyzed except for the movement of a tiny droplet sliding toward her matted hair. "Slip sliding away." It didn't matter what time it was; it was gonna be a long night. The bad events of her life liked to sneak up on her, throw a dark cloth over her head, and hold her hostage until she was gutted by guilt.

Her divorce from Daniel had been a punishing, humiliating failure. A scarlet letter of a different sort—a big red F instead of the familiar A. At least an affair would have meant she'd gotten an A in something. Then there was the issue of the gaping hole left by the loss of her father. If the only man who has ever loved you walks out of your life, isn't it just possible that you weren't enough to keep him there? Usually this litany of regrets was followed by a full-blown self-mugging for the workaholic she'd become.

You're always trying to prove something to someone—you never know when to stop. What are you, a machine? Voices of accusation. Of self-pity. Of regret. She wondered which voice was coming first for her tonight. "Slip sliding away." She straightened out her stiff legs (too much running), untwisted her T-shirt, and hoped desperately that the tears wouldn't overtake her before she could put together some lame rebuttal. Have mercy, she prayed to no one in particular. She curled her body into a tiny, scared ball and waited.

It was strangely silent in room 6-something. The familiar attackers didn't come. No distant hoofbeats, no warships on the horizon. Stillness. And an odd sense of peace. Callie lay there in the dark. Where were the voices? Not that she missed them, but this was most unusual. Who was she to argue?

She dragged herself out of bed, headed to the bathroom, sat down on the toilet, and hung her head. The hotel tile was cold on her bare feet. She blew her nose and stared at the mirror in the dark, seeing way more than she saw in the light—a face too old for thirty-four years. She went back to the bedroom and fished in her black suitcase for socks and pajama bottoms.

Where had the princess gone? Surely her father had lied to her twenty-eight years before. It was that simple. She'd never really been a princess. Daniel hadn't even known what a princess was. And her job gave no allowances for princesses—work, work, and work. She'd become a nine-to-lifer. She'd either been robbed of her princessness, or she'd never really been one. It had worn off. The spell had been broken; the magic didn't work. She sat at the desk there in the dark, wondering, Which is worse, illusion or the death of illusion?

Then a jeering voice echoed in her head. What do you care about being a princess? If you were a princess, you'd just think you had more reasons to be cold and demanding and self-centered. You want your way, Callie, and you don't care what it does to others. Who really wants to be a princess anyway?

"I do." Another voice she hardly recognized creaked out of her throat. "God, please, I do."

Yes, she was talking to herself. Well-acquainted with her own internal monologue, she could have full-scale conversations by herself. But then a new voice interrupted.

"Callie" taking his time with each word, "you are a princess."

It had to be the voice of her daddy. Searing hot pain on her insides gave way to raw longing. Why did you leave me? You called me a princess; you lied to me. I'm no princess! She started crying. Oh, God. Oh, God, help me. She slumped to the floor. I am not a princess. Not anymore. I'm thirty-four years old. Why did you leave me?

"Callie." He took his time with each word. "You are a princess."

Who was it? If it wasn't her father, then who? A strange awareness illuminated her thoughts. Surely not. God? Could it be the voice of God? In a flash, she knew it was. But she didn't believe in God . . . until this very moment. There were many things Callie Randall hadn't believed in until she could no longer disbelieve. She should have been born in the "Show Me State" of Missouri. Still, this time something inside her just knew.

The warm touch of love that had eluded her for so long melted over her heart—the kind of love she had never found within herself. God knows she'd tried hard enough. Or found in the arms of a man—Daniel could vouch for the failure of that one. This world takes; it doesn't give. How can love really be of this world?

Love must come from something beyond us. A yearning she had never been able to express suddenly found a voice of its own. There must be a God, *she thought.*

Then she actually laughed out loud. Who else could call you a princess and really mean it?

All those late-night arguments in bars over the existence of God seemed absolutely silly in the light of the love that was washing over her. New tears began to fall down her cheeks. If there was love, there was also forgiveness for all she'd done wrong. Blessed, quiet acceptance. It felt so good to Callie to cry and then to laugh—so simple and so good. There is a God, *she thought, and although she felt as strange as ever thinking it, she thought that whoever God was, he'd just named her a princess.*

She had no idea when she had stopped crying and laughing and had fallen back asleep on the floor. But when Callie awoke again, the clock said 8:22 a.m. And when she opened the door of room 6-something, she looked directly into the eyes of a man standing across the hall picking up his morning paper. She couldn't have surprised him more as the words tumbled out of her mouth, "I'm a princess."

He smiled slowly and nodded politely while backing through his doorway. It took him a minute to settle on a response. "Congratulations," he said. Still nodding, he quickly closed the door.

Callie never heard him. She wasn't talking to him anyway. "I'm a princess," she whispered to herself back inside her room. This changed everything. She stood straight up, pointed her toes, stiffened her back, and stuck her pinkies straight out. Perfect thirty-four-year-old posture. For the first time since her daddy had called her a princess, Callie Randall felt like one. She radiated love from the nucleus of her womanly soul. It felt so good. So full, so rich.

"Thank you," she said softly from a very deep place. For the first time in years, she beamed. "I'm a princess . . . a princess in my pajamas." Such as they were.

Callie Randall fell asleep that night with the tiara slightly crooked and a lot tangled in her blond hair. It had been a busy day for the princess: flying home across country, returning to a familiar land, negotiating a peace treaty with the rental car agent who had no cars available, returning to the palace to hunt for a very specific treasure buried deep in the attic and found glittering softly at the bottom of the last box she came to. She'd even been an ambassador of goodwill as she telephoned her brother (still not a prince) after ten years of silence.

After all, there was a lot of catching up to do.

★ *Let's Talk about It . . .* ★

- Do you know a Callie Randall? What parts of Callie's story do you find in your own? Can you relate to her struggle and her questions? Are they the questions of every woman's heart if she were honest enough to ask them aloud? Why is the love of God the pivotal piece for her?

- Does it take more faith to convince our hearts we are princesses or to believe that all our desire to be special is somehow wrong?

- In the story, Callie comes to faith, but how would the story be different if she were already a believer? In what ways do women believe in God without knowing his personal love?

- What in Callie's heart responded to her father's name for her? Do we ever outgrow that desire? Why or why not?

- After Callie allowed the love of God to change her heart, she felt she had a lot of catching up to do. Why do you think she felt this?

NOTES

– 1 –

Once upon a Time

IN PREPARATION:

Read chapter 1 of *Keeping a Princess Heart*. To open your time and further your discussion, watch the "Princess Heart" sketch on the DVD of *Keeping a Princess Heart*.

Once upon a time . . . we were little girls. By day we read from our books of fairy tales, and by night we dreamed of the way our lives would turn out. On Sunday nights we parked in our pajamas two inches away from the television. Tinkerbell would fly out waving her wand and putting fairy dust on all the letters on the screen, signifying that the magic was about to begin. The music would swell, and we would hold our breath with excitement as we watched our favorite stories unfold.

Do you ever find yourself these days wondering, what happened? Does it ever seem that somewhere among the prince, the kids, the laundry, and the carpool the fairy-tale company must have been bought out and is now bankrupt? Does it ever feel like life played a cruel trick on you?

Whether we would consider ourselves happy or not, most of us would openly acknowledge that the reality of what we've ended up with is so very different from our dreams. Walt Disney didn't do women any favors, or at least it feels that way on most days. Snow White, Cinderella, and Sleeping Beauty seem to point the way to a life we could never really have, yet it's obviously one we continue hoping for anyway. So let's go back and take a look at some of those early dreams and how they got formed.

✷ Let's Talk about It . . . ✷

- What were a few of your favorite stories from childhood? Do you think the dreams for your life were shaped by these fairy tales or stories? If so, which tales had particular influence on you? Why?

- In what ways were your dreams from childhood realistic or unrealistic? Try not to judge them by the *now*, but try to remember what they meant to you *then*. Was the fulfillment of those dreams a real possibility?

- What are the biggest differences between what you had hoped for and what you are living with today?

- People wrongly assume that these kinds of questions or feelings of discontent only start to surface around midlife. That's often the case, but a crisis is created when loss starts stealing our dreams, no matter what our age is. What were the beginning assaults on your dreams? When was the first time you can remember thinking the world wasn't going to turn out right?

- In an interview with *20/20*, Bruce Springsteen commented that our greatest losses in life happen before we are twelve, and then we spend the rest of our lives trying to deal with them. Why do you agree or disagree with his statement?

NOTES

Some days we feel so far away from our original dreams that we fear we've been tricked and taken to some other life (without our written consent). We think sarcastically, *This is not what I signed up for!* Unfortunately, Walt Disney can't help us with this. He never wrote anything about how to hold on to beauty or hope or grace when disappointment silently slips handcuffs around your dreams and leads them down the steps to a very dark dungeon.

The hard truth is, many of us have watched some of our dreams die before our very eyes—the desperately longed-for child we could never have, the marriage that didn't survive, despite the agony of trying, the illness that stole away a parent or a friend. In the wake of such losses, we seem to have no choice but to trudge on, day after day, through a life quite different from the one we imagined we would have.

- Can you identify a dream that you have watched die? How old were you? What messages did your heart receive?

ꙮꙮꙮ THE WORLD SHOULD HAVE BEEN OTHERWISE ꙮꙮꙮ

Man is the only animal that laughs and weeps, for he is the only animal that is struck with the difference between what things are and what they should be.
—William Hazlitt

Hazlitt is right. The world is not what it should be. We know this deep inside. Singer Natalie Imbruglia put it this way: "Illusion never changed into something real. I'm wide awake and I can see the perfect sky is torn." She's right, too. We are living underneath a very torn sky. On one side are all the dreams of our hearts, and on the other are all the difficult realities of our lives.

NOTES

We are split between what we wanted and what we got
. . . what we hoped for and what we have
. . . what we longed for and what we live with.

DREAMS	REALITIES
Life-long marriage	Painful divorce
Having children	Infertility
Beautiful home	Bankruptcy

What do you find most challenging about living between "what you longed for" and "what you live with"? List some of your dreams and their corresponding realities. Can we dare to hope that there is something more than treading water in the gulf of disappointment between the two?

DOES THE SHOE FIT?

When have you let your heart go to one extreme or the other in trying to make sense of this world? Have you given up trying to make sense of the world at all?

The evidence of this torn sky is all around us. Turn on the radio and you hear a lyric full of love and hope in relationship, and the very next song is full of the hate and rage of having to survive alone. Compare two women's magazines—one will

NOTES

have flowers and beautiful scenery promising the fulfillment of all your dreams, and the other will ditch the flowers, trying to appeal to you, the "smart" woman, by telling you to wake up and take what you want from this world. Go to two different movies in a week. One will be a warm romantic comedy of boy meets girl and the other a cold, crushing drama of a mis-spent life. Below are some examples of these extremes that we find in our culture. List more examples under each category.

MOVIES

ROMANTIC COMEDY
You've Got Mail

CRUSHING DRAMA
The Piano

SONGS

SYRUPY LOVE BALLAD
"Can't Live, If Living Is Without You"

ANGRY RANT
"I Will Survive"

TELEVISION

IDEALISTIC SITUATION
COMEDY
Father Knows Best

CYNICAL SITUATION
COMEDY
Married with Children

MAGAZINES

BEAUTIFUL, PICTURESQUE,
HOMELY
Martha Stewart Living

HARD-HITTING AND
SUCCESSFUL, WORLDLY
Cosmopolitan

NOTES

It's not my wish to frame any of these songs or shows as good or bad, but to point out the mixed messages and the confusion this creates in our hearts. No wonder we feel the tension so deeply—we are in a constant tug of war.

Do you feel the pull? Do you wonder where your heart is supposed to go? The good news is, you're not crazy. And you are not alone in our struggle. Every woman is internally wrestling with the same challenge of how to keep her dreams alive in the midst of life's hard realities. It's the match of the century—the Perfect World vs. the Real World. Which will win our hearts? It's a universal tug of war of spiritual proportions. Every day the back and forth continues, often generating enough force to make us wonder if we will survive.

We will look at the contrast between the "perfect" world and the "real" world more fully in chapters 3 and 4, but a preliminary explanation is important here. Often in our confusion about our hearts, we seek the simplicity of one or the other of two extremes.

CREATING A "PERFECT" WORLD

In a valiant effort to keep our dreams alive, it's easy to hold on to the illusion of our dreams instead. And the difference between the two is enormous. We rightly want to defy the disappointments and pain of the world by trying to create a better world, more like the fairy tales of our youth. But instead of cultivating the good things from the heart of a true fairy tale, we may create a saccharin kingdom of illusion and denial—a pseudo-Eden where we refuse to allow clouds to rain on our parade. We try to stay in the safety of a "Father Knows Best" world, singing love songs, and looking at pretty pictures.

SURVIVING IN THE "REAL" WORLD

On the other side of the torn sky, in our valiant effort to deal with our very real disappointments, we mistakenly give in to the illusion of ultimate disappointment. We rightly want to face our difficulties head-on and not live in denial. We want to grow up and mature. We want to be able to accept the hand that we have been dealt and face our tragedies without sugarcoating them. But instead of facing our tragedies and allowing them to help us mature, we may grow cold and cynical or bitter and angry, creating a private dungeon of disillusionment. This is a pseudo-hell where we won't allow any good to interrupt our misery. We feed this misery by watching TV and film characters that are disillusioned and by listening to the music of other angry women, all the while seeing ourselves becoming more "cosmopolitan."

NOTES

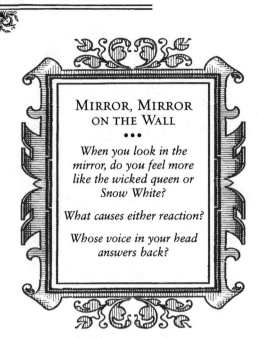

MIRROR, MIRROR
ON THE WALL
• • •
*When you look in the
mirror, do you feel more
like the wicked queen or
Snow White?*

What causes either reaction?

*Whose voice in your head
answers back?*

Of the examples of dreams that you listed above, where does your heart find the most connection, and why? Which extreme are you in danger of living in the most?

If our overarching desire is a meaningful life still full of hopes and dreams, the illusion of a perfect world offers the equivalent of a diet soda to quench our deep thirst. The so-called real world serves up a double shot of Scotch whiskey. Neither is a satisfying choice, but we return to each, time and again. Ask yourself the following questions:

If the "perfect" world is all there is, what happens when I get too weary to pretend any longer?

If the "real" world is all there is, what will keep my heart from dying in such an overwhelmingly brutal place?

Because the illusion of a sugary sweet world looks perfectly positive and the darkness of the so-called real world seems honestly negative, it would be easy to rationalize that together they will balance out each other. But it never works that way. Two halves will never make a whole when both are illusions. Unfortunately we end up like ping-pong balls going back and forth between "fake it" on one side and "get over it" on the other. For our hearts, saccharin or arsenic is poison either way.

NOTES

★ *Let's Talk about It . . .* ★

- In responding to life's disappointments, do you try to control your circumstances, striving for perfection, or do you more commonly become cynical and angry about life? What kinds of disappointments do you find that trigger these responses?

- What are some practical ways we can mature through life's difficulties without becoming jaded on one hand or too idealistic on the other?

While most of us can vaguely sense that both worlds are incomplete, the choices are confusing.

I think we all recognize by now that it wouldn't be so hard to have the heart of a princess if we lived in a fairy-tale world. Discuss for fun for one joyous, unreal minute what that might be like:

The birds would wake us in the morning, we would have beautiful clothes laid out for us every day, a song would always be on our lips, and our good fairy godmother would be there to make certain our dreams always come true. Everyone would love us, and we would love everyone in return. Yeah, right, back to reality.

And in the real world it wouldn't be so hard to give up hope instead of struggling day after day to keep our dreams alive, because in this not-so-fairy-tale world, life is hard. Now discuss what life feels like on the hardest days:

NOTES

We could openly acknowledge that the birds have gone south for the winter and probably died along the way. We could be cynical about everything, be mean to everyone, who cares? After all, we spend our days chained to the washing machine, covered in Cheerios, and on hold with the phone company! Why not admit we're miserable and create misery for everyone else? It's not so unattractive.

Either way wouldn't be so bad, if we could pick our way and live accordingly. But we simply can't be satisfied by living exclusively in either world—both worlds are seductive and dangerous illusions and impossible to live in consistently. So we keep watching, listening, and consuming, trying to make sense of it all. Which world is the most real? As we have discussed, movies, songs, television, advertisements, life experiences all add to the dilemma. They exercise their influence and pull and push. Believe this promise or give up on that dream; let go of that faith or hold on to this product.

- Where do you feel the pulling most deeply?

PICTURE A PRINCESS HEART

WATCH: *Shrek*

READ: *Strong Women, Soft Hearts* by Paula Rinehart (W Publishing)

LISTEN: "Counting on a Miracle" on *The Rising* CD by Bruce Springsteen (Sony)

The difficulty in front of us is finding that place in-between—a place where we can cultivate the true heart of a princess, full of dreams, wonder, delight, and joy, right in the middle of this crazy, broken, hard-to-understand, disappointing world in which we live. This is our real challenge and one I hope this study guide will help us meet.

NOTES

★ *Let's Talk about It...* ★

Whatever faith a woman has will play an important part in determining the way her heart will go, but only if it is a true faith, thought through and lived out. What role can faith play in providing an answer to this challenge? Why isn't faith by itself an antidote to these perfect real/world world detours?

Why aren't Christian women immune to creating perfect world or real world distortions? How does faith become an illusion when it is used to support the false walls of a fake fairy-tale life? And equally dangerous, discuss why the real-world cynicism (full of the ashes of burned-out religion) is impotent in the deeper workings of the heart.

- So, what of the fairy-tale hopes we had? Are they just silly, romantic dreams of foolish schoolgirls? Made-up wishes of spoiled, privileged females who wanted more out of life than life could ever be expected to give? Or might they be the hidden, rarely confessed longings buried in the heart of every woman who walks the earth underneath a torn sky?

- And what of those deep disappointments and sad realities we have had to face? Is that just the way this crummy life goes? Are they crystal-clear examples of why we should never get our hopes up again? Or could they be the harsh instruments that mine the depths of our character and reveal the valuable minerals of maturity?

NOTES

Instead of settling for one of the two extremes, faith shows us another way. It illuminates a new place, an old place really—an invisible kingdom that can only be seen with the eyes of the heart. It's a place where our glimpses of the goodness of fairy tales (that seemed gone forever) can fit into a different view of reality. And it's where the realities of the so-called real world (that feel like hell on earth) are framed in a way that lightens the darkness and removes the cynicism. In this kingdom we can learn how to walk in the glass slipper on broken dreams. We can discover our princess hearts in a place that won't create an unrealistic ideal or collapse into fashionable cynicism.

What we want from life is so much bigger than one road or the other. Carefully, painstakingly we need to sift through each illusion to find the elements of truth. Take one disappointment in your life and walk through the extremes and try to find the way to the middle.

> ### DIRECTIONS TO THE INVISIBLE KINGDOM
>
> ### Psalm 121
>
> *I look up to the hills,*
>   *but where does my help come from?*
> *My help comes from the LORD,*
>   *who made heaven and earth.*
>
> *He will not let you be defeated.*
>   *He who guards you never sleeps.*
> *He who guards Israel*
>   *never rests or sleeps.*
> *The LORD guards you.*
>   *The LORD is the shade that protects*
>   *you from the sun.*
> *The sun cannot hurt you during the day,*
>   *and the moon cannot hurt you*
>   *at night.*
> *The LORD will protect you from all*
>   *dangers;*
>   *he will guard your life.*
> *The LORD will guard you as you come*
>   *and go,*
>   *both now and forever.*

- How might your life look differently if you were consistently trying to find the invisible kingdom and let your heart live there rather than in one of the extremes?

- Do you think we should continue to hope for our dreams to be fulfilled when our circumstances suggest otherwise? Explain.

- On a deeper level, what does your outlook on dreams and disappointments say about how you see God and relate to him?

- How can your faith inform your perspective on disappointment in life?

NOTES

Let's keep going on this journey and see what the next chapter has to teach us on keeping our princess heart. Give your princess heart a royal treat and watch Shrek. Notice the skillful weaving of the concepts we've discussed. You'll find the cynicism and the idealism in a tug of war—decide which one you think wins the day.

WRITE YOUR HEART OUT

In your journal chronicle one big disappointment in your life. Write the story of when it happened and how it affected you. Try to be objective at first about all the details, and then honestly describe how you experienced it in your heart.

The Prayer of a Princess Heart

Father, you know the disappointments we've faced in our lives. You understand the struggle we have faced to make sense of the pain and disappointment that has marked our lives in so many ways. You are not blind to the tug of war that goes on in our hearts threatening to pull us in two. We pray that you would give us the strength to stand with confidence in the space you have made for us in between two worlds of illusion. Forgive us for trying to create our own perfect world apart from you. Forgive us for thinking you have abandoned this world and left us on our own. Instead, gently remind us of your great love that gives our hearts the confidence to stand in the middle of this pulling without being ripped apart. Fashion in us a princess heart. In your name, Amen.

• • • • •

NOTES

WHAT IS ONE THOUGHT FROM THE CHAPTER THAT GIVES YOU HOPE
FOR LIVING IN THIS NOT-SO-FAIRY-TALE WORLD? WRITE HOW
THIS TRUTH COULD IMPACT YOUR LIFE IN THE FUTURE.

– 2 –

Why Fairy Tales Matter

IN PREPARATION:

Read chapter 2 of *Keeping a Princess Heart*.

Read a Grimm Brothers or Hans Christian Andersen fairy tale.

Read the chapter "Listen to Your Longings" in *Fresh-Brewed Life*.

As we dive into this chapter it is important for us to recognize how different fairy tales are from other stories. They aren't just stories for bedtime reading for kids; they are powerful stories for us to read with our adult hearts. Think of the movies that are classic and timeless, the ones that move you every time you watch them. Make a short list of your best ones. I've put down two of my favorites; add a few of your own:

Lord of the Rings

The Princess Diaries

At their core, each of these films have fairy-tale elements that elevate them above normal stories and put them in a category all their own. Let's discuss this idea.

C. S. Lewis wrote that a good fairy-tale "awakens in us sensations that we have never had before, never anticipated having, as though we had broken out of our normal mode of consciousness and 'possessed joys not promised to our birth.' It gets under our skin, hits us at a level deeper than our thoughts or even our passions, troubles our oldest certainties till all questions are reopened, and in general shocks us more fully awake than we are for most of our lives."[1]

Why do you think he made this statement? On what do you think he bases his belief? How have fairy tales gotten a bad reputation over the years? With whom might this have started?

A good fairy tale has three important ingredients: recognition, adoration, and consolation. The details, the names, and the faces all can change—and do, delightfully. Each tale has its own unique characters and plot, and each draws us into the story in a different way. But a classic story will always contain these three important elements. See if you agree.

1. Recognition. The ugly duckling will be recognized as a swan. Snow White's beauty will not remain hidden forever. And Cinderella will finally make it to the ball. In every fairy tale, whenever there is a princess, no amount of rags or dirt or envy from others can keep her from eventually being recognized. She will be found in the end. She will be known.

2. Adoration. The princess will be loved. She may not know it initially. She might cry herself to sleep in utter loneliness, but trust this: Her prince is coming. Sleeping Beauty will not sleep forever. Cinderella will be loved in spite of that awful family. True love is on its way. The prince calls her his beloved, and nothing will stand in the way of his love for her.

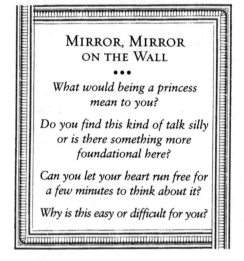

MIRROR, MIRROR
ON THE WALL
• • •
What would being a princess mean to you?

Do you find this kind of talk silly or is there something more foundational here?

Can you let your heart run free for a few minutes to think about it?

Why is this easy or difficult for you?

3. Consolation. All will be well. There are still a lot of obstacles in the story, and at first we can't see how it could possibly work out, but the darkness is going to part, and shimmering light is going to break through. The evil spell will be broken, the cruel curse will be lifted, the sleeping princess will awaken, and the wicked queen will perish. There will be a glorious ending.

I have written that the three elements of fairy tales—recognition, adoration, and consolation—reflect the deepest longings of a woman's heart. It's a pretty bold assertion. Do you believe this is true? If so, how do these three elements connect with your deepest desires? If not, where do they miss the mark in your heart?

NOTES

WHY FAIRY TALES MATTER

FAIRY TALES GIVE US GLIMPSES INTO AN INVISIBLE KINGDOM

When a wardrobe becomes a doorway to another world or a toad becomes a prince, it doesn't take us long to catch on to the fact that things are not always what they seem. When the beautiful sister is actually the ugly one, or when the queen who is supposed to be looking after the castle is wicked and deceitful, everything gets turned upside down. What are some other examples in fairy tales of when things are not what they appear to be? What are some examples of that in real life? How do they compare?

The world of fairy tales sharply reveals that what we see around us is not all there is. There is more, much more. Fairy tales suggest and give glimpses of a very different, invisible kingdom—a world that lives between the illusions of the perfect and the real worlds. Not only is it in between, it is upside down and inside out. In this kingdom, the first are last. The hungry are the ones who will be fed, while those who say they are satisfied go hungry. The ordinary is really the extraordinary, and what others trumpet as extraordinary just might be as common as dirt. Can we truly see this in the world around us, or must we have faith—or some combination of both?

How do fairy tales validate that "the world should have been otherwise" and give us hope for something more?

Why do fairy tales help us bring things into focus, allowing us to see an invisible yet true kingdom between the illusions of the *perfect* world and the *real* world?

NOTES

Why do we need glimpses into an invisible kingdom?

FAIRY TALES AWAKEN DEEP LONGINGS

In the simplest of ways, fairy tales tunnel inside our hearts and spirits; they reach our tucked-away desires for love, truth, beauty, and joy; and they spring them free. Waking us up to dreaming again, they stoke our almost-burned-out desires—desires that are often easier to give up than to live with. Why do women feel that it would be easier to get rid of their desires than to wrestle with them?

1. Recognition. Few adult women would ever admit they desire to be a princess. This is partly because our grown-up hearts dismiss it so quickly as immature and impossible and partly because of the princesses' horrid reputation for being spoiled, demanding, and insecure. You've paid her the highest compliment there is. You've described with one phrase everything her little heart aspires to be. What is your response about that desire? If it was once there, where did that longing go?

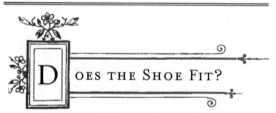

DOES THE SHOE FIT?

A good fairy tale is always dangerous and subversive, because it awakens a yearning or a longing for something more than what is right in front of us. As C. S. Lewis said, fairy tales create a special kind of longing. It is not a longing that makes us despise what we have; it is the kind of longing that creates desire and makes us happy in the very fact of desiring. This desiring is good; it points us in the right direction. This yearning stretches us and lifts us toward what is right, ultimately toward God.

What examples can you give that express "the kind of longing that creates desire and makes us happy in the fact of desiring"?

NOTES

2. *Adoration.* Start talking with any group of women about the idea that one day their prince will come and watch their reactions. You'll get the scoffers and the angry women, who want to fight about men and their role in our lives, and you'll get the dreamy-eyed women, who live in a world of romance novels and soap operas and passively wait to be rescued. But mention the idea to your eighteen-year-old daughter that one day a man might recognize her for the true princess she is, and watch the sparkle in her eyes outshine the Hope diamond. She's not disappointed yet, nor have the delightful myths turned to saccharin. She's still aglow inside with the hope of real love. What is your reaction to someone's saying, "Some day your prince will come?"

3. *Consolation.* Say the words "happily ever after" to six-year-olds, and they will believe in them, even though they don't have a clue yet what "happily ever after" means. Talk about it among women leaders or politicians, and you might be dismissed before the words come out. But mention it softly to the woman in the wheelchair facing the end of her life on earth, and the twinkle you see in her eyes could rival the North Star. Do you still believe in "happily ever after"? What do you think of people who do?

Do you believe that we are most in touch with our deepest desires when we are closest to their fulfillment? Why or why not? Have you given up some of your deepest desires? What will help bring them back?

WRITE YOUR HEART OUT

Describe a time when you have given up because you had no hope. Or describe a time that you didn't give up and held on. What happened and why?

NOTES

FAIRY TALES FAN THE FLAME OF HOPE

I once heard about an experiment with rats. A scientist put three rats in a tub of water to see how long they could swim before they drowned. The rats treaded water for about four hours, and two of them drowned. Before the third one went down, the scientist reached in and pulled him out. He dried the little fellow off and gave him a few days to rest up. A week or so later he conducted the experiment again. He put two rats in another tub of water, along with the one he'd rescued the week before. The little rats started treading water again, and unfortunately around that same four-hour mark the two new rats succumbed to fatigue and drowned. But the other rat, the one that had been rescued before, kept swimming. And swimming and swimming. That little rat swam for two days!

What does that story make you think of in your own life?

Listed right up there with faith and love, hope is one of the top three strongest forces in the universe. And like the other two, hope is dependent upon what it is connected to. Hope is not an engine; it's a hitch. Hope in hope has no power, because hope can't generate anything on its own.

★ *Let's Talk about It . . .* ★

Discuss how the strength of hope lies in what it hopes in. If its strength depends on what it is connected to, what is our greatest challenge with hope?

NOTES

We must understand that we don't hope in the fairy tales themselves; we hope in the fulfillment of the longings they awaken in us. We don't hope that Cinderella is a true story; we hope that one day we will be recognized. We hope that Sleeping Beauty wakes up and that the curse is broken, because we long to wake up from the curse ourselves. As they awaken our longings and reveal the invisible kingdom, fairy tales can help us keep going when we can't see what's ahead. How can Cinderella's story help us keep going today in the midst of all we have to do? What does the story of Sleeping Beauty have to say to modern women who feel they spend most of their lives waiting for something that has never come?

> ### DIRECTIONS TO THE INVISIBLE KINGDOM
>
> LORD, *you know everything I want;*
> *my cries are not hidden from you.*
> Psalm 38:9
>
> *Trust in the* LORD *and do good.*
> *Live in the land and feed on truth.*
> *Enjoy serving the* LORD,
> *and he will give you what you want.*
> *Depend on the* LORD; *trust him,*
> *and he will take care of you.*
> *Then your goodness will shine like the sun,*
> *and your fairness like the noonday sun.*
> Psalm 37:3–6

It is so easy to want to give up before the final act! But wait, let your heart consider this. What if . . .

- even though you are dressed in rags, laboring invisibly around people who don't seem to see you, you are a princess?

NOTES

- even though you think you have given up on love, it isn't over yet?

- even though you can't see how any good could possibly come from the situation you are in, it may well turn out to be the very best thing of all?

Hope says don't just look with your eyes; look with your heart. But how do we do this? What does it mean to see with your eyes? What does it mean to see with your heart?

How can we see with our eyes and our hearts at the same time?

Most of us as little girls loved fairy tales. But today as adult women, facing real disappointments they have never been more important to our hearts. If we will allow our hearts the luxury of opening, these tales will warm us like a crackling fire on a cold night. They can thaw our frozen longings, giving our hearts a chance to feel again.

NOTES

PICTURE A PRINCESS HEART

WATCH: *The Shawshank Redemption*

READ: *Yearning* by Craig Barnes
(InterVarsity Press)

LISTEN: "Legacy" on the *Woven and Spun* CD by Nichole Nordeman

It's because these elements are rooted in the most wonderful tale of all time—the only one that is made more wonderful by the fact that it is true! It is the only story that has the power to change our lives. It is the greatest love story of all time. And if our hearts have grown cold to it, we will miss the best of what life has to offer us. This is why fairy tales matter so much. Their little stories reflect the bigger story of the good news, and once-hidden truths are illuminated for us to see. Like beacons of light across a stormy ocean, they can guide us safely to shores of belief—or rekindle the faith that we thought had burned out. The tales stand in contradiction to the world we see around us and point to the world that is yet to come. In essence, they are a road map to the invisible kingdom.

Let's Talk about It . . .

- How are these fairy-tale elements rooted in "the most wonderful tale of all time?" What difference should that make to us?

- Where do you find these elements in the love story of God?

NOTES

- How can good fairy tales stoke healthy desires in us? What old or modern tales have encouraged healthy desires in you? Should we fear awakening unhealthy desires?

- In what ways can fairy tales lead us ultimately closer to God?

The Prayer of a Princess Heart

Father, thank you for the wonderful gift of fairy tales. These little stories that stirred our hearts when we were young have given way to reveal the grandest love story of all time. But our hearts have grown callous and fearful and even cold as we've tried to deal with all life's challenges. Rekindle our passion and our trust in the things that really matter. Give us a true glimpse into your invisible kingdom. Train our eyes to see your hand at work in this world. Awaken our deepest longings that they might draw us more powerfully to you. Fan the flame of hope in our hears that will keep us from giving up in the midst of this difficult journey when we can't see what's ahead. Fashion in us a princess heart. In your name, amen.

NOTES

WHICH LONGING—ADORATION, CONSOLATION, OR RECOGNITION—
NEEDS TO BE REKINDLED IN ORDER TO DRAW YOUR HEART MORE
COMPLETELY TOWARD GOD? WHY AND WHAT WILL YOU
DO TO MOVE TOWARD THIS LONGING?

– 3 –

Castles in the Air

IN PREPARATION:

Read chapter 3 of *Keeping a Princess Heart*.

I generally have an optimistic view about life, and sometimes I fight the temptation to put a positive spin on things—especially those things I want to be positive. So it's probably no surprise that Christian women are often the first ones accused of building castles in the air. But the truth is, it's a temptation for every woman, no matter her spiritual inclinations. Yes, faith can give a nudge to illusions, but plenty of women can live in fantasy worlds with no help from religion. Turn on any soap opera in the afternoon and see the women of daytime drama floating on a raft of pretense, completely adrift from reality. Magazines of self-help and home decorating have created a church all their own. With wreaths and hot glue and cheap therapeutic advice, women worship by the millions. Take a stroll down Rodeo Drive in Beverly Hills and spot woman after woman climbing strenuously to the top of the "Best Dressed" ivory tower. One glance at People magazine will reveal the lavish attempts to create a fairy-tale wedding for the latest superstar. Women everywhere are pulling out all the stops and pursuing like crazy a make-believe world.

Why would women of faith often be accused of building castles in the air? Is this accusation in any way fair? Why might we be more inclined toward denial than despair?

*Temptation is a suggested short cut to the realization of the
highest at which I aim—not towards what I understand as evil,
but towards what I understand as good.*[1]

—Oswald Chambers

When we are accused of living in a world of denial or of fairy-tale thinking, it's pretty safe to say we went there for good reasons. We want the good stuff. Every woman I know is trying to make her life better in some way—with better communication with her husband, better lawn care for the yard, a better school system for the kids. In what ways, big and small, do you want your life to get better? What are the areas you are concentrating on?

Our hearts were made for faith, hope, and love. But sin corrupts, and as we try to hold the truth with our sin-stained hands we can start to worship faith, hope, and love instead of the God who made them. What happens when we put faith in faith or fall in love with falling in love?

★ *Let's Talk about It . . .* ★

The nuggets of true gold that we gleaned from fairy tales—recognition, adoration, and consolation—provide the breeding ground for great temptations. If we take shortcuts toward our great desires, we run the risk of getting lost in the woods. In *The Weight of Glory*, C. S. Lewis gives a stern warning about the way we hold these things, saying that they are

> Good images of what we really desire; but if they are mistaken for
> the thing itself they turn into dumb idols, breaking the hearts of their
> worshippers. For they are not the thing itself; they are only the scent of
> a flower we have not found, the echo of a tune we have not heard, news

NOTES

from a country we have not yet visited. Do you think I am trying to weave a spell? Perhaps I am; but remember your fairy tales. Spells are used for breaking enchantments as well as for inducing them.[2]

- Why do you agree or disagree with his assessment? If we are made for faith, hope, and love, what happens when we forget God in the equation?

- Where do you most often see this anchorless faith, hope, and love?

We often begin by clutching so tightly the gold nuggets of truth hidden in fairy tales they become disfigured and misshapen images. We take good gifts, greedily cling to them, and even worship them, ignoring the Giver of these gifts. This does not create a princess heart. It does just the opposite—it becomes idolatry that will deform our hearts and make them vulnerable.

Let's look at how we distort these truths and start building castles in the air.

THE DISTORTION OF RECOGNITION

Don't underestimate this powerful desire—it flickers in all of us. Most women labor invisibly, day after day. The majority of things we do no one sees or acknowledges, but the moment someone does see or notice is absolute heaven. We feel as though a veil has been lifted. To be valued and esteemed is one of our deepest longings. We hunger to be known and recognized for who we are—or more honestly, for who we hope we are.

NOTES

Recognition is right. And I don't just mean recognition for accomplishments or deeds, although that is certainly part of it. The greater recognition is in worth and value apart from any deeds, the sturdy confirmation that we are worth more than the sum total of what we accomplish in this life. Like every unknown princess in a fairy tale, we long for our day of recognition. Describe a moment in your life, if indeed there has even been one, when you have felt truly recognized.

Being a princess in the eyes of God doesn't move us toward a princess heart if we worship recognition over worshiping the One who recognizes. In the absence of truly worshiping the King who names us, we are fully capable of fashioning that precious piece of beautiful gold he offers into a little statuette that looks a lot like us. What is the difference between trying to be a princess and trusting that God has named us a princess?

A Distorted Princess: Martha, Martha, Martha

Martha Stewart didn't sell housewares or linens or even canapés. She peddled the illusion of a perfect life. And if her company's bottom line was an accurate indication, we all wanted to buy it. We bought towels and dishes; we bought wreaths made from homegrown vines. We read her magazine, watched her programs, and invested in our own hot glue guns. Why do you think so many women want to be like Martha? What does she represent? Do you ever find yourself wanting to have the perfect life?

How does perfectionism distort the desire for recognition? Why is it ultimately idolatry?

NOTES

We don't take much notice of our idols until they let us down. We feel disappointment when our husbands don't notice the new changes or our mothers still criticize the wreaths, when the kids wipe bicycle grease on the towels and put cat food in the new dishes. Instead of getting what we wanted from Martha, we feel let down and disappointed, and we're not sure why. What were we hoping for, and where did we place that hope?

Idolatry has a law of diminishing returns: The more we get, the more we want. We love our idols when they come through for us, but when they fall off their pedestals and smash into a million pieces, we despise them. If we feel insecure before we buy dishes, we will feel insecure after. If we aren't sure how our husband feels about us, and we buy sexy lingerie to spice up a special evening, chances are good we still won't be so sure about him the morning after. Think about and discuss this statement: *We use our idols to confirm or deny what we already believe is true about ourselves.* Do you agree? Why does the Scripture call this idolatry?

What difference would it make if we believed that personal value is bestowed by God? How can grasping that truth get us off the treadmill of pursuing perfection? How can that belief topple any idol?

NOTES

The Distortion of Adoration

The second piece of gold we can see, thanks to our awakening from the fairy tales, is the truth that we were made for love. Love is right. It is the strongest of all human emotions. Love is the ultimate invitation to life. Always beckoning, love calls to us and says, "Join me—you were not meant to be alone." Life sends us a personal invitation through love, and our hearts quickly RSVP. Whether with a spouse, our children, or someone special, describe how your heart responds when you feel love.

However, the great temptation we face with love is to distort its gold into a little heart-shaped charm. Women become addicted to the feelings of love, and they fall in love with love. Watching love and romance on the big screen, it is easy to worship love's feelings rather than the Giver of all love. How would you explain the difference between the two? Why are women especially prone to the temptation of falling in love with love?

A Distorted Princess: The Marvelous Meg

For a number of years, Meg Ryan was the poster woman for romantic comedies, which I absolutely love—most of the time. The good ones are modern-day fairy tales, and they inspire and delight me. The bad ones are like falling into cotton candy for a couple of hours—you're sticky for a long time afterward. Name a few of your favorite romantic comedies, and list some not so good, cotton candy ones, too.

NOTES

Even the best romantic comedies must be held in our hearts in the right way, or we can miss the joy of real love, for which we were made, and end up in the ditch of sentimentality. Instead of holding the truth "Love means sacrifice," we are treasuring the trite "Just go to a nice dinner and it will all work out fine." We are drawn to the "feel good" part of these movies. We see other people happy and satisfied by the trivial, and we hope it will be enough for us, too. Sentimentality might help a bad-hair day, but why in the deeper issues of life, does it fall miserably short? Give some examples of movies that didn't ring true to real-life experience.

How Sentimental Are You?

Some of us, the romantics at heart, are naturally drawn to sentimentality. Take this quick quiz to check your "sappy" level:

1. How often do you cry at movies?

    ____ Never. I'd have to pluck a nose hair.
    ____ Once in a while when someone dies.
    ____ Every movie has something sad.
    ____ Why don't they just sell tissues at the theater?

2. How many romantic comedies have you seen?
    ____ Meg Ryan? Is she that blond girl?
    ____ One, and I took medication immediately following.
    ____ Only the ones I can trick someone into seeing with me.
    ____ Seen or own?

NOTES

3. How often do you watch programs with angels in them?

    ____ Never.

    ____ I saw a few when my mother was visiting.

    ____ I enjoy watching angels after the evening news.

    ____ We watch them as a group and then have our weekly Bible study.

4. How many things in your home have ruffles on them?

    ____ None. I don't like those kinds of potato chips.

    ____ I have one throw pillow that was a wedding gift.

    ____ Twelve things, not including the dog's collar.

    ____ What's wrong with ruffles? Are you making fun of me?

5. How many romance novels have you read?

    ____ None since high school.

    ____ I started one in a weak moment but never finished it.

    ____ In a week? Or in a day?

    ____ What's wrong with romance novels?

    ____ Okay, I'm starting to see a pattern.

Feeling good is simply not enough for a woman's heart, no matter how romantic she is. If we can't distinguish between love and sentimentality, then when sentimentality fails us—and it will—we'll blame love. Not only is that devastating, it's wrong. If we decide that love isn't worth it or love isn't true, we run the risk of giving up on love. How is that different from recognizing what is and what isn't love to begin with? What are antidotes to a false love?

NOTES

Directions to the Invisible Kingdom

I may speak in different languages of people or even angels. But if I do not have love, I am only a noisy bell or a crashing cymbal. I may have the gift of prophecy. I may understand all the secret things of God and have all knowledge, and I may have faith so great I can move mountains. But even with all these things, if I do not have love, then I am nothing. I may give away everything I have, and I may even give my body as an offering to be burned. But I gain nothing if I do not have love.

Love is patient and kind. Love is not jealous, it does not brag, and it is not proud. Love is not rude, is not selfish, and does not get upset with others. Love does not count up wrongs that have been done. Love is not happy with evil but is happy with the truth. Love patiently accepts all things. It always trusts, always hopes, and always remains strong.

Love never ends. There are gifts of prophecy, but they will be ended. There are gifts of speaking in different languages, but those gifts will stop. There is the gift of knowledge, but it will come to an end. The reason is that our knowledge and our ability to prophesy are not perfect. But when perfection comes, the things that are not perfect will end. When I was a child, I talked like a child, I thought like a child, I reasoned like a child. When I became a man, I stopped those childish ways. It is the same with us. Now we see a dim reflection, as if we were looking into a mirror, but then we shall see clearly. Now I know only a part, but then I will know fully, as God has known me. So these three things continue forever: faith, hope, and love. And the greatest of these is love.

1 Corinthians 13

Sentimentality will not carry us through the hard times in our lives, but real love will. That is why we must be ruthless when we look at our desire for adoration and talk about longings like "someday your prince will come" (we'll talk more about him later). These can so easily be distorted and lead us to the idolatry of love and romance.

Will "romance" be strong enough over the long run to survive an affair?

Will our favorite daytime dramas give us pictures of sacrifice or courage?

What happens when your body has too much sugar? What happens when your spirit does?

NOTES

THE DISTORTION OF CONSOLATION

She paints her world in yellow and green, covering over the gray,
'cause life's demands are hard to understand, so Alice stays lost in her Wonderland.[3]
—Wayne Kirkpatrick

Our desire for consolation is profoundly deep. However, we can also fashion this piece of gold into an idol when we trust the happy ending more than we trust the Author of the play. We make an idol that looks like a great big, cheerful bow. We paste it on the end of every story, of every life, of every day, or even every sentence, whether the Author wants it there or not. We can distort "happily ever after" to mean that everything will have a happy ending, whether or not it really does.

What can the happily-ever-after distortion look like? What are some dangers of rushing past pain to a happy ending?

PICTURE A PRINCESS HEART

WATCH: *Peggy Sue Got Married*

READ: *A Doll's House* by Henrik Ibsen
(Bantem Publishing)

LISTEN: "Alice in Wonderland" on
Angels of Mercy CD by Susan
Ashton (Capitol)

Women are great at writing a happy ending for every story. Part of this is a gift of faith, but another part is How can we tell the difference? Why does it seem easier to simply gloss over things we don't understand?

Have you ever listened to a conversation and overheard someone cheerfully explaining to someone who is in tremendous pain that "Godisworkingallthingstogetherforgood"? Have you ever been hurt by someone pasting a happy ending onto one of your tragedies?

NOTES

In faith, we can believe that ultimately God is bringing all of the difficulties in our lives together in a way that has meaning and purpose, but we cannot presume to understand it all or explain it away so easily.

What is the difference between trusting that there is an ultimate happy ending and making an idol of that ending? How can we stand in the complexity of all that God is working on, not just in the simple part we can see for ourselves?

What can the happily-ever-after distortion look like with a Christian veneer? What are some of the dangers of rushing over pain to paste on a happy ending?

A Distorted Princess: Alice in Wonderland

It is true that the demands of living in a complex world are overwhelming at times. From unclear relationship difficulties to unfathomable global issues, life is terribly hard to understand. But to go around putting cartoon Band-Aids on the gaping wounds of the world is denial. There is nothing more unattractive than a happy face that has been pasted over a grimace of pain.

Read the Christmas letter from *Alice in Wonderland* (of *Keeping a Princess Heart*) and discuss the implications of this story.

Our Unfinished Stories: Talk Amongst Yourselves

Women have a God-given capacity to ignore pain and allow love to cover a multitude of sins. But what happens when we knowingly give the illusion that everything is just fine when it so clearly is not?

Mirror, Mirror on the Wall

• • •

The tables are always set beautifully in castles in the air, but look closer to see that the paint is peeling badly. Alice is leading the way to denial, Meg is pushing us toward sentimentality, and Martha is cracking the whip of perfectionism—each touching something in us that is very real: our deepest desires.

NOTES

We are never promised that everything will have a happy ending. We are not even promised that we will live to see all the joyous turns we long for. Our sons may not give up their drugs, our neighbors might not recover from cancer, but we have been given the promise that we haven't seen the ending yet.

Which stories in your life are unfinished at this point in time? What ending would you like to see come about? Can you hold your happy ending in your heart and yet yield it if necessary to trust the Author?

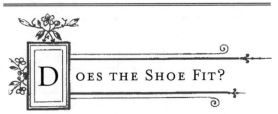

Does the Shoe Fit?

Which of the women representing the distortions do you identify with the most—Martha, Meg, or Alice? Why?

Coming Down from the Castle

It's easy to confuse the longing for the ultimate happy ending with the illusion of that temporary "happily ever after." We were created to be loved, so it's understandable that we could fall in love with love. And it is our God-given desire to be recognized that tempts us to seek our own recognition. But faith, like a fairy tale, creates wonder, never illusion. It inspires and delights; it doesn't deny and sugarcoat. We long to live in the truths revealed by fairy tales, not in the illusion of living the fairy tales themselves. The truths offer freedom and the illusion, pure slavery.

NOTES

How can we balance our good desires for our personal lives without becoming bent toward them, being controlled and trying to control?

It would be nice to blame Martha, Meg, and Alice for the way they have led us astray, but it's not their fault. The illusions are seductive on their own, because they call out to the deepest places within us. But allowing those desires to become idols of worship instead of altars of sacrifice will indeed break our hearts. Instead of the life we wanted, we get a life as thin as a temporary Hollywood facade. And like the best in Tinseltown, it's a very expensive front—costly in more ways than one.

Isn't it time we came down from our castles in the air?

The Prayer of a Princess Heart

Father, we need your help to keep a princess heart in a not-so-fairy-tale world. It's too easy to breathlessly chase after the world's recognition by seeking to impress everyone. Can we quietly trust that you have called us a princess? Forgive us for giving in to entitlement thinking and at times acting demanding and spoiled. Show us the power of real love that rises above the sentimentalism that never satisfies. Keep our heart from pretending that everything has a happy ending when it so clearly does not, and help us put our trust in you, the God of history, who promises us that one day all will be well. Fashion in us a princess heart. In your name, amen.

•　•　•　•　•

NOTES

WHAT LIGHT CAME ON IN THIS CHAPTER THAT MIGHT HELP TO
ILLUMINATE WHETHER YOU HAVE BUILT A CASTLE IN THE AIR?
WHAT STEPS WILL YOU TAKE TO COME DOWN?

– 4 –

Dungeons in the Dark

IN PREPARATION:

Read chapter 4 of *Keeping a Princess Heart*.
Watch the sketch "Raising the Sail" on the *Keeping a Princess Heart* DVD.

Many of us can remember the very day that we first tasted the bitter pills of disappointment and unfulfillment. What we may not remember so well is what we decided to do after that: accept this or keep trying to understand? This is so important. How do we keep our hearts from learning the wrong lessons from our disappointments? In the last chapter, we looked at the difficulties created when we make idols of good things. Putting too much belief in one particular part of the truth distorts that truth. But turn the gold coin over and notice the flip side. Disbelief. Not assigning *any* value to those same truths. Rather than elevating the truths in the fairy tales into idolatry, we subjugate them to the realm of pathology. We see them as a disease—something wrong in our hearts that needs to be removed or an illness from which we need to recover. Let's spend our time together in this chapter looking at what we've done with our disappointments and what our disappointments have done to us.

Is it possible that not putting enough belief in the truth also distorts it? If we define truth only by what we can see, feel, and touch, we limit our belief out of fear and pain, which can create an equally devastating distortion. What are the dangers of defining truth only by our own experiences and feelings?

Which extreme, the castle or the dungeon do you tend to move toward more often and why? Before we venture into the world of the dungeon, try taking this little quiz to discover the shade of your jade:

1. "Happily ever after" is a myth . . .

    ____ only during my period.

    ____ almost every day.

    ____ since 1941.

2. Someday my prince will come . . .

    ____ about 5:30, after work.

    ____ but he got lost on the way and wouldn't ask for directions.

    ____ yep, he came, and now he's in the other room, watching TV.

3. If there were a glass slipper . . .

    ____ I would try it on for fun.

    ____ I would assume it doesn't come in my size.

    ____ I would fill it with rocks and plants and make a terrarium.

4. My biggest dream is . . .

    ____ a richer life.

    ____ more money than bills.

    ____ a good night's sleep.

5. If seven dwarfs showed up on my doorstep, I might . . .

    ____ invite them in for tea.

    ____ act like I don't speak English.

    ____ call the exterminator.

NOTES

Why is the last option in each of these questions so appealing?

Most women want to be smart and real-world minded. We don't want to be Pollyannas in other people's eyes. But what is the difference between sadness over the ways things have gone awry and anger that we ever hoped for anything different? What is the difference between not getting something that you want, and thinking that nothing ever works out for you?

There is a fashionable (and often understandable) cynicism that pervades our culture. Where do you find it in your heart? When did you first notice it, and when does it come up most often? (In relation to your marriage? To your kids?)

When I think of all the longings that are unfulfilled for most women, when I think of all the things that never come to completion for many of us, it breaks my heart. Many of these longings will remain unresolved until heaven, but that doesn't mean we deny them or kill them. With so many heartbreaks and so much sin in the world, our answer has been to put our hearts through a training course in disappointment management, which ultimately acts like a lobotomy.

NOTES

★ *Let's Talk about It . . .* ★

- Which is the greater danger, our hungers or a soul that is no longer hungry for anything?

- Why is hope a necessary ingredient to many enjoyable qualities of life, such as wonder, nobility, imagination, and beauty?

- What are some dreams that you have given up on? How have you handled the disappointment?

- At what points in your life does a cautious or fearful voice inside you say, "Don't get your hopes up"? What would happen if you allowed yourself to hope again?

- Our longings are boundless, and we need them. Thank goodness our hearts are not small. Our desires are not predictable. We cannot be figured out easily. Why doesn't this feel like a good thing?

NOTES

- Is God embarrassed or worried by this because we're so complicated?

- What does it say about God that he welcomes our deepest hungers and our strongest questions?

DESCENDING TO THE DUNGEON

Many of us live in private prisons of our own making. Because of disappointments, bad choices, or impossible circumstances, we relegate our hearts to the dark hold below. When in England, I took a tour of Warwick Castle and got an education in dungeon dwelling. I saw historic, gruesome instruments of torture that were once used to impose the will of the state on wayward men and women. But even today, I recognize them because they still exist in our world. People continue to use them in various forms to torture others. Sometimes, we even use them on ourselves.

INSTRUMENTS OF TORTURE

Oubliette. This is a beautiful French word with a terrible definition. It is the word for an ugly, deep, dark hole where prisoners were abandoned—forgotten for good. It's sort of like solitary confinement, only worse. It is every woman's greatest fear—abandonment. No one sees, and no one cares. Haven't you been there? You fear that whatever you've done (or whoever you are) is so bad that no one is ever coming for you again. You're totally alone. And somewhere in your mind you're afraid you deserve it.

The scolding bridle. This was a hard metal harness that was fitted over prisoners' heads, and they were led around the city while others shouted insults at them for the crimes they had committed. In the old days, proof was rarely required for an alleged crime. A woman (or a man) could merely be accused of something and be punished accordingly. Deeds done (and just as many not done) would be announced to all the world, and the accused would be on public display, dragged around in front of everyone in the scolding bridle of shame.

NOTES

The hanging chains. This horrific device was a skeleton of metal that covered more than half of the prisoner's body. It hung from the right corner of the dungeon, suspended in midair. An accused criminal would be fitted in these chains and left to hang until death provided release. People sometimes completely broke down just being measured for this brutal device. Once in the chains, the victims hung above the prisoners in the dungeon, forced to look down at the mobility of the others. Their emotions were as tortured as their bodies.

Which of these instruments of torture sound most familiar to you and why? How do we use these implements on ourselves?

The Denial of Recognition:
"You're No Princess!"

It is easy for any voice of truth to be drowned out by the whispers of Warwick. Our deepest disappointments often become our darkest dungeons. The whispers of the oubliette, the scolding bridle, and the hanging chains don't go away on their own. Left unchecked, the whispers ultimately become louder and more strident. Far from living out a fairy tale, we descend deeper and deeper into the dungeon.

In your own private dungeon, do you ever just slump against the wall and listen?

- The oubliette whispers, "Forget being recognized; you are forgotten."

- The scolding bridle whispers, "Forget being recognized; you have no worth."

- The hanging chains whisper, "Forget being recognized; you can only watch others get what they want."

NOTES

★ *Let's Talk about It...* ★

- Do you think that it is easier to believe we are not special or to trust that we are?

- How can a woman struggling with infertility find herself in the dungeon? How might being single feel like the oubliette? Or being in a difficult marriage? Can you identify the way that women lead themselves around in a scolding bridle of shame and self-criticism?

- Why might we make our disappointments even darker by blaming or punishing ourselves? What do you think God thinks about this self-punishment?

If the gold of this truth is not made into an idol or fashioned into a weapon, it can be forged into a key that will unlock our darkest dungeons. Here is the gold key: You have been recognized. Your crimes were enough to put you in the dungeon, but you were not forgotten there. The King has thrown open the door and stepped in to find you. The scolding bridle of shame and guilt has been broken and destroyed. You are loved. Your worth is not determined by your deeds; it is granted by your Father. Your guilt is cleansed by forgiveness. The chains of envy can be melted away by gratitude. Your heart can be free, able to grow strong once again.

NOTES

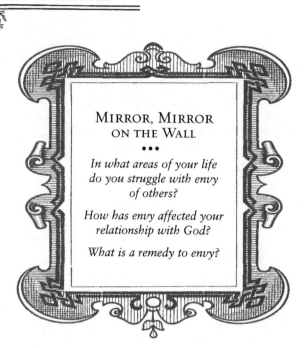

MIRROR, MIRROR ON THE WALL

• • •

In what areas of your life do you struggle with envy of others?

How has envy affected your relationship with God?

What is a remedy to envy?

In what areas of your life do you need that key to unlock your dungeons?

THE DISMISSAL OF ADORATION: "THERE IS NO PRINCE!"

I believe that the most lawless and inordinate loves are less contrary to God's will than a self-invited and self-protective lovelessness.[1]
—C. S. Lewis, *The Four Loves*

If we become so cynical about the idea that any man could ever be a prince, then we resign ourselves to the dungeon of lovelessness. Diametrically opposed to the idealism of making too much of love is the cynicism of not making enough.

Love hurts and disappoints us many times over. That's the truth. That's the awful, painful, heartbreaking truth. But to say that love always hurts and disappoints is plain wrong—and self-defeating. Or to imply that because we have not found the love we are looking for, it therefore doesn't exist is equally untrue.

Read aloud the mock fairy tale on page 79 of *Keeping a Princess Heart* and discuss. What can laughter conceal in our hearts?

NOTES

Women don't end up in the dungeon of lovelessness for no reason. Very real wrongs have stolen some of the most precious things from us. Many disappointments will never be made right. In the awful crimes of sexual or emotional abuse, there is a dark irony that can understandably lead to despair. The offender looks free on the outside while the one hurt ends up in the dungeon, racked by self-hatred and fear. Women who have suffered at the hands of another often keep their hearts locked up their whole lives.

How can we know whether our hearts are locked up? What does a heart in the dungeon look like? How does it respond to life's joys and challenges?

WRITE YOUR HEART OUT

It can be painfully difficult to acknowledge the dungeon. Sometimes what we do to our hearts in private is hard to share. How cruel are you to your own heart for its longings and desires? Do you punish it for your disappointments?

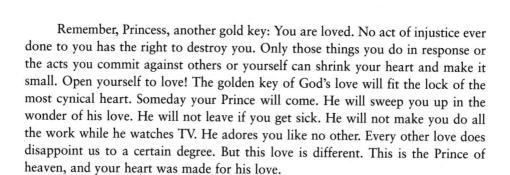

Remember, Princess, another gold key: You are loved. No act of injustice ever done to you has the right to destroy you. Only those things you do in response or the acts you commit against others or yourself can shrink your heart and make it small. Open yourself to love! The golden key of God's love will fit the lock of the most cynical heart. Someday your Prince will come. He will sweep you up in the wonder of his love. He will not leave if you get sick. He will not make you do all the work while he watches TV. He adores you like no other. Every other love does disappoint us to a certain degree. But this love is different. This is the Prince of heaven, and your heart was made for his love.

NOTES

The Death of Consolation:
"All Will Not Be Well!"

It is hard to believe in "happily ever after" anymore. And a lot of people don't. They believe it lost the election in the recount or it got destroyed in the document shredder. Just reading the paper is enough to make most of us think there is no happy ending to be found. At best it is a myth that makes us feel good. At worst it is a lie that should be exposed.

What Walt Disney did to the fairy tale on one side by making it too perfect, countless film directors have done on the other side by dragging it through the dirt. They make movies and parade them out as the latest version of "reality," when in truth their pictures are propaganda for a world without hope.

You are made to feel foolishly naive if you don't subscribe to their unhappy, hopeless conclusions. When have you felt this during a movie? What were you watching? Have you ever left the theater more confused and troubled than when you went in?

Does the Shoe Fit?

*When we encounter suffering, we often ask, "Why is this happening to me? Why do I deserve this?" The **why** questions can be just as punishing to our hearts as thumbscrews or shackles. Do you believe that we ought to fully understand the reasons behind our situation or suffering? The castle in the air offers pious explanations, while the dungeon just gives callous responses like, "Sometimes you win, and sometimes you lose." Where is the road in the middle?*

Some of these films are a reaction against the saccharin sweetness of an unrealistic "happily ever after," which is understandable and right. But often the stories go way too far to the other side by promoting a worldview of despair and futility. Name films on both sides of this dilemma and which ones you think have found a balance in between.

NOTES

Examples: The difference between endings in these movies or others you can recall:

- *The Parent Trap* and *Step Mom*

- *When Harry Met Sally* and *The War of the Roses*

- *Beaches* and *The Divine Secrets of the Ya-Ya Sisterhood*

Okay, so life in the castle oversimplifies, but the underground dungeon intensifies life. It makes every issue so complex that there are no suitable answers. Doubt arrives like a storm, and despair settles in behind it like a dark cloud. We give our hearts room to believe that there is nothing and no one guiding the universe, and ultimately life is never going to turn out right.

Remember, Princess, a third gold key: All will be well. We have a promise that the King is working things out in the world that we can't see. We will cry now, we will not understand it all, we may think we'll never make it through the storm—but he promises he will never leave us or forsake us. He helps us go to sleep at night with a stronger sense of the power of good and an understanding that he is protecting us from evil. He hasn't assured us that we will always get our way; he has promised that he is the Way. And in his way, despite our suffering, we can safely trust that all will be well.

> ### DIRECTIONS TO THE INVISIBLE KINGDOM
>
> *How do the stories and parables in the Bible turn out? Read Luke 15:11–32. What kind of ending is found in the parable of the prodigal son? Does it give in to an unrealistic "happily ever after" or to a dark futility threaded with despair? Discuss.*

COMING UP FROM THE DUNGEON

If we can acknowledge that what we see in the world is not all there is, we are strengthening our eyes of faith. We can live clinging to the good even when it feels like our fingers are getting rope burn. Whatever we do we can't let go of the truth.

NOTES

In the dungeon, the way out isn't found by lowering our expectations. The way out is through letting the keys open the doors to free our hearts and allowing them to soar upward, toward the goodness they were created to hold.

How can a woman guard her heart wisely without imprisoning it? How is it possible to be realistic about evil and still maintain hope for the future? What promises of God do you find particularly encouraging?

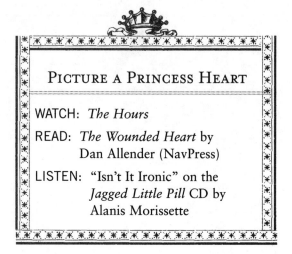

PICTURE A PRINCESS HEART

WATCH: *The Hours*

READ: *The Wounded Heart* by Dan Allender (NavPress)

LISTEN: "Isn't It Ironic" on the *Jagged Little Pill* CD by Alanis Morissette

The Prayer of a Princess Heart

Father, help us to understand that having a princess heart does not make us Pollyanna, but neither does it make us a perennial pessimist. Don't let us take either fork in the road. Guide us straight ahead through the middle, no matter how uncomfortable it gets. Let your love pull us down from the castles in the air and keep us above the dungeons in the dark. Let us never forget—we have been recognized. We are loved. And one day all will be well. Walk ahead of us to clear the path through the middle of the forest and beside us to keep us on the right course toward the invisible kingdom. Fashion in us a princess heart. In your name, amen.

• • • • •

NOTES

WHICH INSTRUMENTS OF TORTURE WILL YOU HAND OVER TO CHRIST
SO HE CAN BEGIN TO FREE AND HEAL YOU? WRITE ABOUT WHAT
YOU HAVE LEARNED THAT WILL HELP YOU DO THAT.

– 5 –

The Invisible Kingdom

IN PREPARATION:

Read chapter 5 of *Keeping a Princess Heart*.
Watch the sketch "The Invisible Woman" on the *Keeping a Princess Heart* DVD.

Although there are exceptions to almost every rule, I find that women generally tend to gravitate to emotional extremes. We often laugh about this together because we know it to be true. We are either full of hopes and dreams, excited about the future, or we can't get out of bed because we're convinced that nothing is ever going to be right again. On good days we poke fun at ourselves, bouncing back and forth. We can start the day in the castle, whistling while we work, and finish the day crying in the dungeon, certain that our lives are over. Does this ring true for you? Why is it especially challenging for women to stand in the middle rather than move toward emotional extremes? Do you think that men find it easier to maintain a position in the middle?

Doesn't it feel as though the dungeon of the real world seems to force our eyes wide open? With twenty-four-hour news coverage on television stations, the Internet, radio, and newspapers bombarding us with images of horrific events, we often see much more than we want to. Very often I feel completely overwhelmed. But on the other side of things, our castles in the air call us to keep our eyes closed tight against all the evil. This is where the invisible kingdom is going to show us another way. It's going to call us to open the eyes of our hearts. This kingdom says to us, "Look at the world honestly, but don't think that what you can see with your eyes is all there is to see." There's a different world going on, concealed behind the clamor and confusion on the surface.

Before we go further, reread the two sections in chapter 5 of *Keeping a Princess Heart* called "Princess of the People," and the "Princess of the Poor."

Let's Talk about It . . .

- Where were you the morning of the Royal Wedding in 1981? What feelings did it evoke in you?

- What do you make of Mother Teresa's statement to Diana, "To heal other people you have to suffer yourself"?

- How would you describe the way Mother Teresa saw the world? What allowed her to see things this way?

DISCOVERING THE INVISIBLE KINGDOM

Opening the Eyes of Our Hearts

In what ways can fairy tales sharpen our ability to see the unseen kingdom? How are they a reminder to delve deeper than our circumstances?

NOTES

Which is more real, the seen or the unseen? Which is a family more hungry for, the Thanksgiving food shared around the table or the connection of their hearts amid the feast? What is more real for the young mother who changes diapers all day? Does the unseen joy of caring for her precious baby rise above the smell of dirty Huggies?

If you were to view the disappointments of your life with the eyes of your heart, instead of what you see with your physical eyes, what would look different? How is viewing things this way more than Pollyanna thinking?

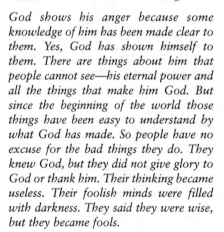

DIRECTIONS TO THE INVISIBLE KINGDOM

God shows his anger because some knowledge of him has been made clear to them. Yes, God has shown himself to them. There are things about him that people cannot see—his eternal power and all the things that make him God. But since the beginning of the world those things have been easy to understand by what God has made. So people have no excuse for the bad things they do. They knew God, but they did not give glory to God or thank him. Their thinking became useless. Their foolish minds were filled with darkness. They said they were wise, but they became fools.

Romans 1:19–22

When people look at a mountain, some see only a mountain and others see the majestic handiwork of God. With eyes of faith we can recognize the invisible attributes of Creator God, who fashioned a beautiful world. What are the challenges in looking at the world with eyes of faith?

NOTES

Embracing the Hidden Strength of Humility
Why is humility a key characteristic in the invisible kingdom? How should we handle our desire for recognition?

Many people broadcast their good deeds and hide their bad deeds. We find then that what lives on the inside of a person becomes the total of all the things they are hiding. In a sense, we are as sick as our secrets. A woman's heart then can be full of the badness tucked away from the rest of the world.

But consider this: What if the greater way to live is to hide your good deeds and openly confess your bad? We know that the strength of a good deed done in secret is increased. When you have done a good deed publicly, you are openly applauded and admired, receiving your credit and any reward right then and there. Then it evaporates. But what if we decided to hold the good things inside where others do not applaud? Would the negative things that are confessed, then evaporate? Would the good multiply instead of the bad?

Finding the Beauty in Invisibility
Read the following story of the invisible woman:

It started to happen gradually. I would walk into a room and say something, and no one would notice. I would say, "Turn the TV down, please." And nothing would happen, so I would get louder. Finally I would go over and turn the TV down myself.

Then I became more and more aware of it. And not just with the kids. It happened with my husband, too. We had been at a party for about three hours, and I was ready to leave. I looked around and saw he was talking to a friend from work. I walked over, and he kept right on talking. He didn't even turn toward me. That's when I started to put it together: He can't see me . . . I'm invisible!

Suddenly I saw it everywhere. I walked my son to school, and his teacher said, "Who is that with you, Jake?"

"Oh, nobody."

Nobody. Granted he's five, but it's not just him.

NOTES

I work to put dinner on the table, and no one acts like anybody put it there. Everybody sits down, and my husband says, "There's no butter." Which means, "I can't see you, and I'm not even addressing you, but when I say there is no butter, the butter lady will get up and get it." Presto, the butter appears, and on we go. No one knows how their socks get back in their drawers, how their favorite treats end up in that mysterious brown bag by the door, who comes to pick them up after school, or why the dog doesn't wet on the rug anymore.

No one sees me. My teenager takes everyone else's advice but mine. My husband talks to other people like he's interested and doesn't even ask me about my day. My preschooler wants to play, but I'm just a body to roll over with the trucks. I am invisible. In a crowded room, no one can see me. I'm just a mother in the grocery store like every other mother, looking for the coupon items. I'm just a wife at a business dinner with every other wife who is bored to death but happy to be out of the house.

WRITE YOUR HEART OUT

Did you ever feel invisible as a child? Did your parents see you? What about your friends? Do you ever feel invisible in your own life today? What are some things that you do that no one ever notices?

VALUING HIDDEN EFFORTS

There are amazing similarities between the builders of the great cathedrals and motherhood.

No one can list the names of the people who built the cathedrals. Thousands of people gave their lives to build a monument to God. But there is no record of who they were—no plaques, no certificates, no praise.

They devoted their whole lives to a work they would never see finished. Many of the cathedrals took more than a hundred years to build. That was way more than a working man's entire lifetime. Someone could start work on this great building knowing he would never live to see what it would ultimately become.

They spent time on details that would never show. When one worker was asked why he was spending time carving the figure of a bird into a beam that would be covered over by the roof and no one would ever see, it is reported that he replied, "Because God sees."

NOTES

They made great sacrifices for no earthly credit. They had to trust with eyes of faith that what they were doing mattered. They believed the finished work they were helping to create would stand and bring glory to God, which, if you've ever seen them, you know they do.

Discuss the similarities you see between motherhood and the builders. Even if you don't have children, what are areas in which you work that no one seems to see? How do you think the Lord sees hidden efforts, such as many things mothers do? What are some beneficial side effects of being invisible?

MIRROR, MIRROR ON THE WALL

• • •

Any woman seeking to be a princess will live alone in the visible kingdom surrounded by "stuff" that others can see. But a woman cultivating a princess heart will live invisibly, trusting that there is more to life than what can be seen. She is a citizen of an invisible kingdom. An insecure princess will flaunt her good deeds, but a princess heart will keep them quietly at home. A spoiled princess might demand to be first, but a princess heart is free to be last, confident that she is loved. Do you find your heart living more for the visible kingdom or the invisible kingdom?

How do you understand our "dual citizenship"? What would it mean to live as a citizen of the invisible kingdom? How might that look in our daily lives?

If you close your eyes and listen, you might be able to hear God saying something like this: "I see you; you're not invisible to me. I see the sacrifices you are making. I see your tears of disappointment. You may feel invisible to those around you, but you are never invisible to me. I miss nothing. No act of kindness, no task, no cupcake, no sequin sewn on is too small for me to notice and smile over. You are building a great cathedral. Keep building. You can't see it now, and it will not be finished in your lifetime. You will not have the chance to live there, but if you build it well, I will."

What would it mean in your life if this were how God feels?

NOTES

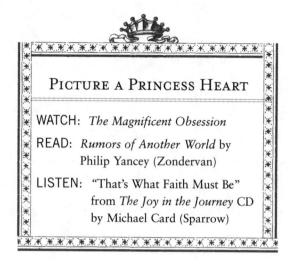

PICTURE A PRINCESS HEART

WATCH: *The Magnificent Obsession*

READ: *Rumors of Another World* by
Philip Yancey (Zondervan)

LISTEN: "That's What Faith Must Be"
from *The Joy in the Journey* CD
by Michael Card (Sparrow)

The Prayer of a Princess Heart

Father, sadly we understand that life is never going to be perfect in the here and now. But don't let our hearts use that as a reason to give up. Show us the life you have carved out for us between our young idealism and our midlife cynicism. We confess that we can see life only through a dark glass. We have some light, but we can't see everything. Forgive us for when we have not trusted you, because we only know in part. Increase our faith that we might let go of the past and stop trying to predict the future. Remind us that we don't have to pretend with you, nor do you expect us to quit trying to understand. Give us the strength to stand in the invisible kingdom between the "no longer" and the "not yet," seeing the world through the lens of faith. Fashion in us a princess heart. In your name, amen.

•   •   •   •   •

NOTES

WHAT ONE TRUTH ABOUT THE INVISIBLE KINGDOM RESONATED
IN YOUR HEART? AND HOW WILL YOU ALLOW THAT
TRUTH TO SET YOU FREE?

− 6 −

You Are a Princess

IN PREPARATION:

Read chapter 6 of *Keeping a Princess Heart.*
Watch the DVD or video of Walt Disney's *Snow White and the Seven Dwarfs.*

She is standing on the tarmac of the LAX runway with a baton in her hand helping to bring my plane to the gate. I'm watching her, and she's watching the wheels and the wing of the aircraft while motioning it forward with the stick. It seems like an invisible job to me, and I wonder if she minds it. She has beautiful, long, dark hair, and I wonder if she ever doubts her beauty. I wonder if she hears compliments from her friends. I wonder if she laughs freely and loudly or if she's quiet around her family. I wonder if she goes home after work to someone who adores and appreciates her. I wonder if she works with people who think she is special. I wonder if she knows God has named her a princess. I silently pray that if she doesn't, she soon will.

The Scottish preacher and poet George MacDonald saw the world quite differently than most of us. He saw every woman as a beautiful princess dressing down on the outside as an ordinary mother or lawyer or teacher. He believed that in the invisible kingdom, the greater strength of people came from what was in their hearts, as opposed to anything that was in their wallets or in their closets or on their résumés.

Can you see the mark of the invisible kingdom? The world sees ordinary people going about their days and tasks and recognizes a few extraordinary ones when they dress up on the outside in remarkable clothes or noteworthy accomplishments. But the invisible kingdom turns that inside out and challenges us to look deeper.

Do we dare believe such good news today? That every woman is a princess walking in this world with that kind of identity? What could that mean to a woman's heart? How would belief in that truth change her thoughts, not to mention her spirit and her relationships?

THE PRINCESS CONFUSION

We get a lot of mixed messages in the world today about what a princess is. The very word *princess* is in danger of going the way of other beautiful and meaningful symbols trying to survive in a world of image. Our symbols—Princess is only one example—have a tendency either to become remote and unattainable, except for the privileged few, or they become so common that they are cheap and tawdry.

Of course we've all seen T-shirts and bathrobes, halter tops and thongs emblazoned with the word Princess, sometimes even in rhinestones. But its use on these items is just a word, not a name. What it means is so cheapened by its commonness that it has nothing to offer us. Far from elevating the idea of the princess, the culture tattoos it everywhere but on the one place it matters the most: our hearts.

* What does the word *princess* make you think of?

* What happens to a symbol, such as a princess, when it is elevated beyond our reach? What are the implications for those who reach for the unattainable? for the woman who thinks that she has attained it?

* On the other hand, what would be the motivation for cheapening a symbol, reducing it to the lowest common denominator?

* How do you react to the statement, "What we can't attain we level"?

THE PRINCESS FACE

When symbols are separated from their deeper meaning, either by being placed out of reach or cheapened to irrelevance, then only the image of the thing is left. And in these days image is everything. So what are the differences between having a princess heart and putting on a princess face?

NOTES

The face of where we live has changed the face we live with. Life used to be lived in small towns in the country, and now it's moved to the large cities and their suburbs. People often live in twenty different places over their lifetime and sometimes work almost as many different jobs. We've literally left face-to-face relationships that were stable and consistent to make fast, superficial, largely anonymous acquaintances. Where does character find its place in all this? If a first impression is the only impression, where have we decided to put our effort?

I love the writing of Erma Bombeck. With titles like *If Life Is a Bowl of Cherries, Why Am I in the Pits?* She tackled the issue of getting older by pointing out the difficulties we all face. She made us laugh out loud as she gave words to help us see that the wrinkles on our faces, the bumps on our noses, small lips, sagging breasts, and the general spreading out of everything were realities of this earthly life to be borne with dignity and humor. She taught us to laugh about the things we couldn't change.

But no longer, it would seem. It's difficult to make jokes about any of these things because they are changeable. You can get your nose done, your breasts enlarged, and your tummy tucked, so where is the humor in our aging these days? Our culture shows us that these things are changeable and shows us how to change them. That makes us responsible and even considered foolish if we don't do something about them. Why do you agree or disagree?

Cosmetic surgery started as the humane treatment of wartime injuries. Today it is a multibillion-dollar industry that is practiced mostly on those in good health. The number of people going in for surgery has tripled in the last ten years. And, surprisingly, the largest percentage of those going in for the most popular procedures—nose jobs and breast enlargements—are between the ages of nineteen and thirty-four. Why are you surprised or not surprised by these figures?

The word *cosmetic* is defined as something used or done to cover up defects. And this raises some interesting questions: Are wrinkles really defects? Do we see small breasts as a fault? Has age become a flaw? Then why do these things need to be covered up or corrected? We used to think of flaws in terms of a person's character, not a person's appearance. Nowadays, no one seems sure which is worse, immorality or crow's-feet.

What lies at the root of the dramatic upswing in cosmetic surgery and its absurdities within society?

NOTES

What evidence do you see that society prizes eternal youth?

What does that mean to the natural aging process?

What question do you think plastic surgery provides the answer to?

If you were going to have a part of your appearance altered, what would you have done and why? What would change with the procedure? What are the dangers as you see them?

Or perhaps you have already had cosmetic surgery. Did it turn out like you wanted?

Is it possible we are dragging down our hearts as we lift up everything else? What kind of pressure do you feel in society regarding your appearance? Is it easy for you personally to let those messages roll off or is there a deeper struggle there?

NOTES

THE PRINCESS HEART

For as [a woman] thinketh in [her] heart, so is [she].

Proverbs 23:7 KJV

Snow White was the fairy tale that started it all. In 1937, Walt Disney produced the first animated motion picture, but the story was published by the Grimm brothers in 1812 and illuminated perfectly the age-old conflict between image and heart. How do we daily face this conflict? Do you think that women ask a question of their mirror every day? Why do you think women compare themselves all the time? What does that do to our hearts and spirits?

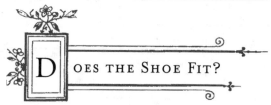

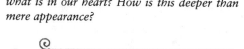

DOES THE SHOE FIT?

An older woman with a princess heart can watch Snow White at any age, without envy, if she still sees herself as the one with dreams and hopes. But if our hopes have died and we've covered hardened hearts with beguiling images and constant comparisons, it's far harder to identify with Snow White and far easier to envy those who are still young and innocent and dreaming.

What do you think the Bible means when it says that as we think in our hearts, so are we? How does our face accurately reflect what is in our heart? How is this deeper than mere appearance?

Some women have criticized fairy tales for their portrayal of women. They have pointed out that it seems like all the old women in the stories are ugly, mean, and cruel while the good characters are all young, beautiful, and innocent. But they misunderstand the fairy-tale world. Isn't it the condition of our hearts that determines which character we identify with? Is the queen wicked because she's old? Why is Snow White described as lovely?

NOTES

WHAT'S IN A NAME?

Let's talk for a moment about what names mean to us. Almost everything has a name, and if it doesn't, we give it one. We name our children, our pets, and our stuff. People name things they love in order to claim them and care for them. Our children name their dolls and toys. A name gives dignity and value. If you have children, how did you decide what to name them? If you don't have children, what other names have you picked for people or pets that were significant to you? Why were they significant?

It's hard to recognize the value of a name in our present culture, because what we *do* seems more important than who we *are*. But what you do is not who you are; it's only a label. Beautician, agent, lawyer, mother—none of these is your name. Why don't we just name people by what they do? Why don't we assign people a number?

> ### DIRECTIONS TO THE INVISIBLE KINGDOM
>
>
>
> *From the ground God formed every wild animal and every bird in the sky, and he brought them to the man so the man could name them. Whatever the man called each living thing, that became its name.*
>
> *Genesis 2:19*

Why would it matter to be named a princess by God?

We are namers, because God was a namer. He brought Adam into existence and gave him his name. Then God allowed Adam to name the animals for him.

A name asserts that a new life is beginning, a new identity is coming into being. When God called Abram to himself, he gave him a new name, Abraham, and promised him that he would be the father of many nations. When priests or nuns take their monastic vows, they choose a new name to signify a new life.

NOTES

_____

_____

_____

_____

_____

_____

_____

_____

_____

_____

_____

_____

_____

_____

_____

_____

_____

_____

_____

_____

_____

_____

_____

_____

_____

_____

And very interestingly one chapter later after the Fall, Adam is hiding among the trees in the Garden of Eden. The Lord calls directly to Adam. He says, "Where are you?" God didn't say, "Human being that I have created, come out of the bushes!" He spoke to him personally. He had created him and knew him as Adam. He spoke to him as Adam. God has done this since the beginning of time. The unique value and dignity of human life came from our Creator. While the Bible is full of all those genealogies that we like to skip over, they demonstrate the importance of our names in the eyes of God.

Named by God

Who can give a woman this, her own name? God alone. For no one but God knows and delights in who she is, and who she will become.[1]

—George MacDonald (paraphrase)

Regardless of whether we know him, he knows us. God tells us that he knew us in our mother's womb, that he smiled at our birth, and that he knows everything about us. He tells us that he sees our aspirations and our dreams and our struggles. God tells us that he knows us even better than we know ourselves. And best of all, he knows something beyond what we know: He knows what he is calling us to become.

Heaven holds its breath as God speaks a name that is deeper than our gifts or abilities; a name that gives us our place and purpose in the world. For a woman, it is a portrait of her heart and soul, which belongs only to her and to no one else in the same way. It expresses the nature, the character, and the life purpose of the woman who bears it.

No one but God can recognize you fully.
No one but God can love you so completely.
No one but God can fulfill your heart's deepest desires.
No one but God can name you Princess.

Despite today's distortions, the princess has been the most adored figure throughout most of history. Royal, beautiful, and admired, she holds the hopes and dreams of her country in her heart and in her smile. Not yet a queen, her life is rich with possibility and promise and, one day, a throne. Daughter of the king, loved by the people, sought by every prince in the land. With beauty and poise and strength, she bestows honor and grace. She is confident and radiant and courageous.

NOTES

Believing Our Name

Let me know you, for you are the God who knows me; let me recognize you as you have recognized me. You are the power of my soul; come into it and make it fit for yourself, so that you may have it and hold it without stain or wrinkle.[2]
—Augustine, *Confessions*

God calls us Princess because that is who we are before him. It's not a make-believe, flattering word meant to buoy our spirits so we don't wake up depressed every day. But, naturally, it lifts our spirits and changes our perspective and helps us rise above doubt and depression. To be named by God means to know who we are and to be free to be who we are. Free from the past to start over. Free to become what he has in mind for us.

How is a name more than a symbol for a person, but rather it is the person?

The princess heart is our invisible nature as a member of the royal family. It is never a badge or a label to slap on in public. It is a secret name that acts like a passport to an alternative world, in-between the castles in the air and the dungeon. It's not a T-shirt or a bumper sticker or a set of assumed manners. What happens to its real power if it becomes any of those things?

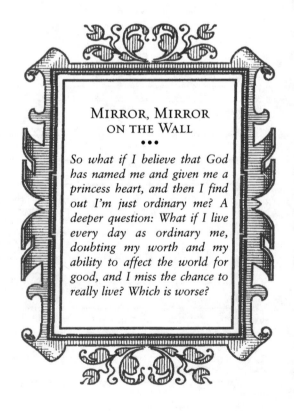

Mirror, Mirror on the Wall
• • •

So what if I believe that God has named me and given me a princess heart, and then I find out I'm just ordinary me? A deeper question: What if I live every day as ordinary me, doubting my worth and my ability to affect the world for good, and I miss the chance to really live? Which is worse?

NOTES

What is your greatest obstacle to believing you are a princess? What would it mean for you to respond to God's calling you to become your name? How does the princess heart fit into the invisible kingdom? Why is secrecy important?

He names us before we were born, and only he sees who we will become. And at every opportunity given to him, he whispers it again and again to our hearts. "Princess . . . you are a princess."

From my window seat I glance once more at the tarmac at LAX. The princess is still standing there disguised, dressed down in her ordinary work uniform. And despite the commercial earplugs she is wearing, I hope that today will be the day she hears the King whisper her name.

PICTURE A PRINCESS HEART

WATCH: *Roman Holiday*

READ: *Forever Erma: Best-Loved Writing from American's Favorite Humorist* (MJF Books)

LISTEN: "This One's for the Girls" from the *Martina* CD by Martina McBride (RCA)

The Prayer of a Princess Heart

Father, teach us how to stake our hearts, like young oak trees, on the claims we believe to be true. Help us spend our greatest energy, not on proving these claims, but on growing up, supported by their strength to become exactly the women that you have made us to be. Let us live without concern for our own image or reputation. Let us live for the approval of the One who named us, the One who recognized us. It is your recognition that matters, not our own. It is your renown that we are after. Our own accomplishments need not be trumpeted anymore—we know they don't create our worth; that is settled by our name. Teach us not to fret over our faces, because they are a reflection of our hearts, not the definition of our value. Set us free, gloriously free to be ourselves as you see us. Fashion in us a princess heart. In your name, amen.

• • • • •

NOTES

HOW HAS YOUR NAME AFFECTED THE DIRECTION YOUR LIFE HAS
TAKEN SO FAR AND HOW MIGHT YOUR LIFE CHANGE, KNOWING
GOD NAMED YOU WHAT YOU ARE TO BECOME . . . PRINCESS.

− 7 −

Someday My Prince Will Come

IN PREPARATION:

Read chapter 7 of *Keeping a Princess Heart.*
Watch the DVD or video of Walt Disney's *Cinderella.*

Standing in the kitchen in a tattered bathrobe, she rinsed out her coffee cup. The kids were on the bus with their lunches, her husband was stuck in commuter traffic, and the dog was looking up at her, waiting for his food. If you had asked her, she wouldn't have even known she was humming as she opened the dog-food can. But a smile might have played across her lips if you had told her she was humming the tune of "Someday My Prince Will Come."

Every good fairy tale has a prince—Prince Charming, Prince Wesley, Prince Caspian. Many have no name at all—they are simply referred to as "the prince." But in almost every story, no matter his name, he goes about doing two things: finding and rescuing. These are the tasks and the joys of a prince. He will find the princess and rescue her from her situation: lovelessness, boredom, poisoned apples, or sleeping disorders, to name only a few. As we begin this chapter on the love of a prince, name a few princes in modern day fairy tales.

THE ROUNDTABLE

Read this paragraph and discuss the questions:

Women are strong, capable initiators, and we can hold our own in almost every situation. We are determined, forceful, and talented. But when it comes to love, we want a heart to respond to. We don't want to sweep; we want to be swept away. We don't want to catch, as much as we want to be caught up. We like to draw, but not as much as we like to be drawn in. We may search, but our hearts long to be searched for. We want to be looked after, talked to, turned on, thought about, and prayed over—all of which amount to responding rather than initiating. We may be modern women, but our hearts are still full of timeless desires.

1. Is the description of a man as a finder/rescuer and a woman as a responder an outdated stereotype or is it a timeless insight into the heart? Explain.

2. How do the desires for love of a man (finding and rescuing) and a woman (responding) fit into the modern context?

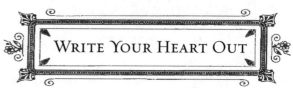

WRITE YOUR HEART OUT

3. What does it mean to be "found"? What powerful influence can this have on a woman?

Did you ever run away from home? Why did you leave and where did you go? What did you hope would happen? Did you ever hide and hope that someone would come looking for you?

4. Describe your feelings and impressions as you read the story of Cinderella afresh.

DOUBTS ABOUT THE PRINCE

If you've watched the story, you know that *Cinderella* is a classic tale of a little girl, seemingly invisible to those around her, who finally comes into her own. She is treated cruelly by her stepfamily, and then she is discovered by a prince. He is so taken with her that he turns the kingdom upside down to find her. The prince takes

NOTES

her away to a glorious life in his castle where she is finally treated like the princess that she is . . .

Ahem, back to real life . . . Cut the music. The story is over. Let's come back to earth now . . . We all have laundry to do.

As we watch or discuss this story, if our hearts explore too deeply into the story of Cinderella, something inside cuts us off. Is this just reality kicking in, or is it the dungeon and our doubts? Sure, love might begin like that, we tell ourselves, but it won't last. Or we think, that's not how it turned out for me. Our cynicism comes up from the dungeon and refuses to let us cooperate with the notion of being so deeply loved for two reasons: First, because we've never known a prince like that. Second, because we've never been loved like that. Let's explore these two reasons more fully.

WE'VE NEVER KNOWN A PRINCE LIKE THAT

For the record, men deserve a book of their own dedicated to keeping the heart of a prince in this not-so-fairy-tale world. They have their own difficulties finding their paths. How does a man continue to value character and virtue and nobility in the midst of a culture that seldom praises him for much beyond his image?

In his book *The Image*, Daniel Boorstin wrote, "It used to be that a man was famous because he was great; now a man is seen as great because he is famous."[1] The contrast of those two is staggering. Before television, the public image of a man didn't contribute anything to his greatness; it was merely a by-product of the greatness that was there. But now a man (or woman) becomes a celebrity by appearing in the newspapers, movies, television, and, our most recent addition, on the Internet. People who have done nothing to achieve real greatness are famous simply because they are recognized. Figures who never would have had fame are now in the media every day. We notice that their lives are empty of real achievement, but they are not known for real achievement. Instead, they are well known for their well-knownness. The celebrity has taken the place of the hero in our modern world.

THE HERO	THE CELEBRITY
A timeless figure	A flash in the pan
Described in sacred texts	Described in magazines and movie screens
Defies mere public opinion	Defined by public opinion
"A big man"	"A big name"

NOTES

Discuss men who might fit into the categories listed below and why you think they're celebrities or heroes.

TV "Bachelor"   Firefighter

Movie star   Police officer

Politician   Math teacher

Musician   Father

What impact has this phenomenon had on the hearts of men? on heroism?

This antihero is a relatively modern protagonist celebrated for having no heroic characteristics nor fame or fortune. We've championed his "nothingness" brought out in sitcoms and movies. When tragedy strikes, the antihero makes us laugh by running away, even knocking people down to get out first. The antihero models the road to destruction, showing men what it looks like to lose hope, to give up, or to destroy their lives with addictions they are powerless to overcome. Who (in TV or movies) are examples of the antiero? Add to the list . . .

TELEVISION   MOVIES

George Kastanza, *Seinfeld*   Nicholas Cage, *Leaving Las Vegas*

How did your impression of "the prince" get formed early on? Who did you think he would be? Where has that impression had to change? When has it given way to disappointment? What about joy? Who, if any, are the true princes you have known?

NOTES

WE'VE NEVER BEEN LOVED LIKE THAT

The second reason we find it hard to identify with Cinderella's prince is because many of us have never been loved like that. Why would a woman trust a love that she has never known? How could she? Better to just get on with the errands and stop daydreaming. Far better for our hearts to leave the happy story of Cinderella to the little girls and get back to business or to dismiss Cinderella, as a poor misguided girl who just wanted to be the center of attention than to allow ourselves to imagine that we could be the one at the ball.

But don't you think Cindy must have had her doubts, too? She must have faced the same battle in her spirit that we all do. I like thinking about her doubts because it helps mine.

As she was racing home and the clock was striking midnight, each toll of the bell took something away from her. The pumpkin carriage smashed into pieces. But wasn't it a magnificent carriage just minutes ago? The coachmen returned to their ordinary form of mice and scampered into the night. Were they really coachmen, or did I dream it? Then, looking down, she noticed she was back in the same rags as before. Plain old Cinderella. Where had the princess gone?

Here's where the battle comes in.

What would she do to her heart the next day? Would she allow deeper doubt to creep in? Would she question whether she was really ever at the ball? Was it too good to be true? Was it just a dream? "How could I have been so stupid? How do I go back to my real life and forget what just happened? What was I thinking? I'm no princess! I'll never be loved. Look at the way I'm dressed. Look at all this work I have to do!" She could land herself in the dungeon in no time.

Or she could climb the steps to a castle in the air by arrogantly marching into her stepsister's room, taking some of the clothes out of her closet, and claiming them for her own. She could have now thought, *After all, I am a princess. No, you don't see it, but you should have seen me last night. Everyone loved me. I was the talk of the ball—the prince noticed* me, *not* you. She could now demand that her stepsisters treat her better. She could have put on a princess T-shirt and announced that princes from all over would soon be beating down her door.

NOTES

★ *Let's Talk about It...* ★

Take the following situations and describe the extremes of the castle in the air and the dungeon in the dark.

- You have been trying to get pregnant and think that this time maybe you have.

- You are single and have met someone new in your life.

- You have a difficult marriage, but experience a wonderful evening with your husband.

- In your job, for the first time, your boss recognizes the work you are doing and says so.

Where will your heart live? What doubts will come and what will you do with them? Where will you put your hopes and dreams?

Cinderella may have had deep questions the days after her evening at the ball; the story doesn't say. But she had one thing that helped her deal with the doubts, enabling her to stay out of the dungeon and away from a castle in the air. Cinderella

NOTES

had a shoe. For whatever reason, everything had turned from the extraordinary back into the ordinary and wretched, except for the glass slipper. The slipper was still real. So Cinderella tucked it away and continued as before. She had no idea what would come next, but she knew she was different on the inside. And when she doubted, she could look at the glass slipper and know it hadn't been a dream. She had danced with the prince in that shoe, and she would never be the same. The hidden glass slipper was only *one* shoe—not strong enough proof that would ever convince the world. But Cinderella didn't need to convince the world—she needed only to remind her heart.

How can we remind our hearts to trust? What can we look at, or look to in our everyday lives that would tell us, "Remember, you are loved; you have not been forgotten; your life matters, and there is a prince who loves you"?

Through his practice, Paul Tournier, the Swiss psychologist, saw many women as modern Cinderellas. He saw them as heroes of unmarked devotion, exploited by everyone all their lives. Invisible, with no one paying any attention to them as persons. Trampled upon, they sit alone in the ashes of sadness and doubt the value of their existence. Feeling as though they are only here to perform services for others, they have no idea what they really want in life. Tournier found great joy in playing the part of the fairy godmother by reviving a "Cinderella" who had been crushed since childhood. By recognizing her, he could begin to speak tenderly to her heart and send her out to meet the real prince. Do you connect with Tournier's analysis? Who is a

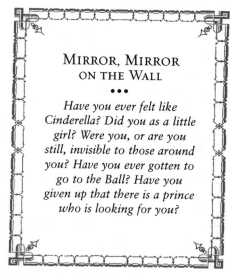

MIRROR, MIRROR
ON THE WALL

• • •

Have you ever felt like Cinderella? Did you as a little girl? Were you, or are you still, invisible to those around you? Have you ever gotten to go to the Ball? Have you given up that there is a prince who is looking for you?

NOTES

modern-day Cinderella that you know? Are we all modern Cinderellas in our hearts? Is it possible that we are like the little girl sitting in the ashes, that we are often unable to see what can become of our lives until we meet the prince?

Meet the Prince Who Loves Like That

Check out the passage in the Scripture Luke 7:36–50. Read the biblical account first and then the following story. I have taken some liberty, but I think you'll see the point.

He was at a friend's house when she came in. She was a mess. She'd been crying and couldn't hold it all together. She had to walk by people in the house to find him. She could hear their whispers, "What's she doing here?" The other women were more than curious—"Who is she looking for?"—each afraid it might be her husband. But she just kept on until she saw him.

Then she couldn't keep from sobbing. She couldn't speak, but there was no need for words. It was obvious what she was saying. Everyone in the room knew the woman kissing his feet was for sale. Perhaps some of the men had bought her before and felt nervous with her there. They wanted him to stop her from carrying on. One man standing near the scene was thinking, If this man were a prince, he would be able to recognize a princess, and she ain't it.

But the invisible kingdom reveals a different version.

She walked in the door, and all of heaven fell silent. The dancing ceased. The violins stopped playing. All eyes rested on the rare beauty of this unknown woman. She had been found.

The whispers started immediately. "He sees her."

As she approached him, he alone could see into her heart. He alone knew what God had named her. He alone could feel the pain of where she had been. And despite her tears, he alone could see the beauty she would become. He knew she was a princess because she was a daughter of the King. The Prince recognized her, took her by the hand, led her out on the floor, and danced with her in front of everyone.

NOTES

Mouths fell open. The crowd couldn't fathom the kind of love that would cause the Prince of all heaven to dance with a prostitute princess.

This is the kind of love that finds and rescues. Finally, our Prince has come!

How does thinking of Jesus as the Prince affect your desires to be known and loved? In what ways is the Prince of heaven the truest prince? What is this Prince able to see in the weeping woman that the others don't recognize? How might this influence how you relate to an earthly prince?

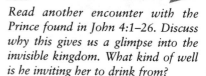

DIRECTIONS TO THE
INVISIBLE KINGDOM

Read another encounter with the Prince found in John 4:1–26. Discuss why this gives us a glimpse into the invisible kingdom. What kind of well is he inviting her to drink from?

YOUR PRINCE WILL NEVER BE A PRINCE

He was on his cell phone in Starbucks. I was at the next table, which put us two inches apart, so I heard more than I wanted to. "Why do we have to go into this right now?" There was silence as she spoke. "Can't we discuss it when I get home?" I wondered if she would give. "I know, but I've got to finish the report by two."

She decided not to wait until he got home, and she launched into arguing and laying out her case. I could tell because he slightly rolled his eyes and waited . . .

NOTES

"Yes, I am upset. I just show it differently." Silence again. "Don't cry . . ." And then, "Why are you so mad at me?" Long pause. "I'll be home around two thirty . . . I know I said two, but we've been on the phone for thirty minutes, and I have to finish this report by two. I don't want to talk about it anymore. I'll be there as soon as I can." He hung up the phone and hung his head.

The woman at home will probably never know this, but he cried.

Somewhere along the journey we stopped hoping that the prince would come and started hoping that the prince would come through. The hope of his physical presence changed into a demand for his emotional presence.

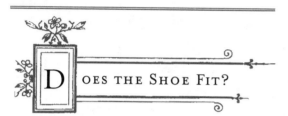

Does the Shoe Fit?

Have you ever been the woman at home on the phone? Do you ever put pressure on your husband or your boyfriend to be the Prince? How does he react or respond?

Most every woman seeks to get the love she needs from an earthly prince, but at some level it will not satisfy her—ever. The thirst for love in a woman's heart must be met first by a higher love, from a well that won't run dry. Unfortunately, an earthly prince just doesn't have that much water.

And neither does a princess. A princess can't make a man a prince by marrying him, any more than she could put him in the garage and make him a car. Marriage doesn't determine a prince; it reveals him. Sadly, many a princess has married a toad that stayed a toad. And equally sad, just as many princes have married beautiful women they thought were princesses, who never turned into anything but demanding.

How does a princess's knowing her name help solve this dilemma? What will keep her from clutching the prince by the throat, emotionally, to get her needs met? In what ways does knowing the real Prince take the pressure off the earthly princes?

NOTES

PICTURE A PRINCESS HEART

WATCH: *The Princess Bride*

READ: *The Sacred Romance* by John Eldredge and Brent Curtis (Thomas Nelson)

LISTEN: "Goodnight to a Mother's Dream" on the *Flyer* CD by Nanci Griffith

The Prayer of a Princess Heart

Father, thank you for sending us such a beautiful picture of your love. Because of the Prince, our hearts can be set free to rest in our belovedness. And when we doubt, as we are so prone to do again and again, cause us to look at the glass slipper on our dresser. We have it—a strong visual reminder of your presence. It's still there. Yes, you love us. We don't have to prove it or show it off or wear it for the world to see. We need only to trust in our name and in your love and keep walking. And when someone asks us, "Hey, Cinderella, does the shoe fit you now?" We can answer with the confidence your love has given us, "Yes, by grace, it does indeed." Fashion in us a princess heart. In your name, amen.

· · · · ·

NOTES

HOW WOULD YOU FEEL TO KNOW THAT NO MATTER WHERE
YOU HIDE OR IN WHAT DUNGEON YOU FIND YOURSELF
IMPRISONED, GOD WILL COME LOOKING FOR YOU?

– 8 –

Happily Ever After

IN PREPARATION:

Read chapter 8 of *Keeping a Princess Heart*.
Watch the DVD or video of Walt Disney's *Sleeping Beauty*.

As we enter our last chapter of this study, it's appropriate that we're looking closely at the happy ending. But sadly, all too often our life experiences do not successfully add up to "happily ever after." People we love have died, circumstances have devastated us, evil has won stunning short-term victories over good, and we have been left with doubts about love's ability to conquer all. Yet even after being buried under questions or submerged in fear and cynicism, the most timeless desire of our hearts has a way of bobbing to the surface, glimmering with hope.

She tumbled into bed about midnight and finally fell asleep, wishing the world were a better place, wishing there were more good news to report, and most of all, wishing the kids hadn't watched an earlier newscast with her, which had included a terrorist bombing, a murder, and the kidnapping of a little boy.

Now it's three thirty in the morning, and her four-year-old is patting her on her arm. He is sniffling softly. She sits up in bed, trying to focus on his face in the dark. "What is it, honey?" The little boy remains silent. She reaches for her bathrobe at the foot of the bed, picks him up, and heads down the hall toward his room. As she lays him back in his bed, his crying intensifies. She asks again, "What is it?" His little lip quivers, and he looks toward the wall, not wanting to say. "Are you scared?" she suggests. He nods and cries harder. "Can you tell me? Do you know what you're afraid of?" He shrugs his shoulders.

She takes her little son into her arms and kisses the top of his head. "It's okay," she whispers into his hair. "Whatever it is, it's going to be okay." She holds him, lost in her own thoughts. Is it really going to be okay? Can I promise him that? Should I tell him Mommy wonders the same thing sometimes?

She has calmed his fears so easily, so confidently—so instinctively. In her heart she deeply believes "all will be well," but in her head she isn't quite sure how she can promise it. She looks lovingly at her son, who has finally fallen asleep, snuggled in the warmth of her reassurances. And she pads back to her own room, praying for some reassurances of her own.

Does this story resonate with your heart? Have you been there and even asked some of the same questions? Is a mother's instinctive "it's going to be okay" a sugar coating of the facts for a child or does it speak of a deeper truth beyond the immediate circumstance? Explain.

At the very center of human life is a deep trust in the order of things. If we didn't have this trust, we would not view the ultimate outcome of our personal stories as loving or joyful or peaceful but as terrifying. Without some innate sense of order, we would never be able to reassure our children, "It's going to be okay." But we can offer this reassurance, because deep inside our hearts, we hold a strong hope as people of faith: that death does not have the final word, that evil will not ultimately win, and that love will conquer all.

This is the deepest longing of our hearts: the desire that all will be well.

The Beauty of Sleeping Beauty

The story starts happily and innocently with the birth of Princess Aurora. But when the evil sister of the king is not invited to the baby girl's christening, the trouble begins. The day of celebration comes, and the friends and family speak blessings over the little princess. Then the jealous aunt arrives. She blows in like a dark cloud and pronounces a curse before anyone has a chance to stop her. She decrees that the princess will prick her finger on a spinning wheel and die before her sixteenth birthday. Needless to say, the celebration turns dark, and happiness turns to mourning.

NOTES

One of the other aunts steps in. While she cannot undo the curse, she can cancel the power of death. She declares that when the girl pricks her finger, instead of dying she will fall asleep. It will be a sleep like death and will last for a hundred years. But at the end of that time a king's son will come and wake her, and she will live. In the meantime, all the others vow to do their best to protect the princess and make sure she never pricks her finger. They decide to tuck her away for safety and to rid the kingdom of all spinning wheels. Everyone feels a little better, and the party resumes.

Life goes on in the castle for years, and the curse is all but forgotten. The princess continues to grow and become more beautiful and kind. Then, on her sixteenth birthday, just as predicted, the princess pricks her finger and falls asleep.

There is terrible sadness in the kingdom. A few remember the old curse and are able to explain to the others what has happened, but that provides little comfort. Even if the curse is only for a hundred years, the daughter is still gone. For who will live long enough to see her again? Meanwhile, how many people do you think told the king that his beloved child would never wake up? Or how many implied that he was in denial because he believed that she would?

Time passed, and around the castle it grew harder for anyone to remember the princess at all. Some parents passed on the story to their children, but few believed the promise that the spell would be broken after a hundred years. The ones who did believe had no proof, and others gossiped that they were crazy. Once the king died, no one kept count of the years at all, and the world just kept on going. Those few who still remembered knew that whatever might happen wasn't going to happen in their lifetime, so they might as well give up. It looked as though all was lost.

What are the parallels between the world of Sleeping Beauty and our world today? Who is sleeping and how did they end up that way? Have we lost count, or worse, lost hope that our curse will ever be lifted?

NOTES

THE IMPORTANCE OF THE ENDING

When we can't see the present meaning, the future ending takes on a greater importance. We think, *How will all this turn out? If I can't see the reasons in the short term, show me what I'm missing by giving me the long view. I can understand the meaning if I can see the ending.* Women don't say, "Show me the money." We say, "Show me the ending. Don't leave me hanging. Show me where this is going, and then I'll agree to go. Just don't ask me to trust in the dark." We women will go almost anywhere and bear almost any burden if we understand why we are doing it. You want us to wait—we'll wait, but first tell us what we are waiting for and what it means. We can bear almost any "how" if we believe in the "why."

Why is meaning so powerful in our lives? How can we still have hope when we might not grasp the meaning? What "hows" have you borne because you understood the "whys"? Why do you think the endings are so important to us? Why is the ending not as important to men? Or is it?

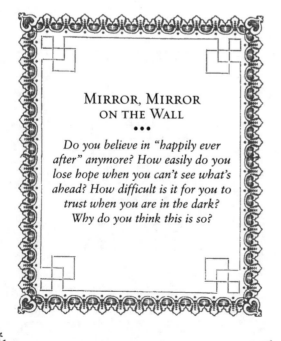

MIRROR, MIRROR
ON THE WALL
• • •
Do you believe in "happily ever after" anymore? How easily do you lose hope when you can't see what's ahead? How difficult is it for you to trust when you are in the dark? Why do you think this is so?

Anyone can write a fake happy ending by giving each character what he or she wants. Likewise, any author can finish a story unhappily by killing everyone off. But the true artist, according to screenwriting coach Robert McKee, is one who "gives us the emotion he's promised . . . but with a rush of unexpected insight" that he has withheld

NOTES

until this turn at the end. The insight that pours forth delivers the longed-for emotion in a way we never could have foreseen. Yet McKee insists that the clues were there all along. The best endings have been threaded through the story from the beginning.

Revisit from chapter 4 your favorite movie endings. Look at your list again and discuss what made the endings great.

- Can you see the clues to the ending planted deep within the story? Why does the ending make or break the story?

- What about bad endings? Give some examples of those.

Tolkien describes how fairy tales usually end so well, often bringing us to a "sudden joyous 'turn'" that in the face of horrific events "denies . . . universal final defeat." This is why we love them. They give us "a fleeting glimpse of Joy, Joy beyond the walls of the world, poignant as grief."[1] Tolkien believed that fairy tales' power lies in the fact that they resonate the true story of Christ's passion and resurrection—the greatest, most complete, most inconceivable, and joyous turn ever.

NOTES

But back in the story of our world, the perfect sky is still torn. Our "once upon a time" seems long ago and far away. Today's world faces wars, diseases, hunger, and poverty. We see power struggles between political parties and watch institutions created to end abuse harbor the abusers themselves. And when we can't see the meaning, the ending takes on a greater importance.

But amid all the darkness, we can still be people who wait with hope. We can hold on tightly to our longing that good will triumph over evil in the most glorious ending imaginable. We have good reason: The Author of history has been whispering it to us since the beginning of the story. And throughout the centuries, the Author has continued to sprinkle clues of what we can expect. In essence he is saying, "Wait, don't give up. Look at what's ahead." He has been foreshadowing parts of the greatest ending of all time.

What are some of the clues we find in Scripture that might reveal a part of the ending? Like *Sleeping Beauty*, what are some stories in Scripture that tell of hoping for a promise to be fulfilled beyond a lifetime? What are some lessons for us in these true tales? In what ways do fairy tales "resonate the true story of Christ's passion and resurrection"?

The Ultimate Ending

There are three key points to remember when we think about the ultimate ending of our personal story:

1. We can't see it all from here. We've grown used to seeing everything at once. We want to walk into life as if it's a great room and be able to see it all in an instant. But real life is never that way. It is far more like an English cottage, unfolding and revealing itself over time. Because we can't see it all from here, we have to trust more than we like to. Why does this trust make us uncomfortable?

NOTES

2. *We can't see it all now.* Humanity is stranded in time. We have organized our days into hours and minutes so that we can see change as it occurs. Apart from the need to mark change, there would be no need for time. But God does not operate in our time because he never changes. He does not set his watch by Greenwich, nor is he bound in any way by its constraints. Likewise, he does not view history the way we do, in terms of past, present, and future. Every moment is always the present for him. We view the events of our lives in chronological order because of our understanding of time, but these events are not put in that same order by God. He has the ending in mind at the beginning and the beginning in sight while the ending is unfolding. How can understanding this bring comfort to our hearts in the midst of difficult circumstances?

3. *But we can see something.* Just because we can't see it all at once and we can't see it all now doesn't mean that we can't see anything at all or that we should give up. Our limitations shouldn't make us give in to this kind of postmodern thinking: "You can't see it all, so you might as well stop looking. You can't understand the concept of time, so quit waiting for anything. You don't understand the meaning, so that proves there is none." This is why there are no postmodern fairy tales. There would be no love, no hope, and no "happily ever after." They would never satisfy us, because our hearts know that there is so much more.

Why is postmodernism like "high-fashion clothing . . . very difficult to wear in everyday life"? What examples have you seen of its inconsistencies?

NOTES

All Will be Well

So how can we as women believe in a happily-ever-after ending when there hasn't been a happily-ever-before? We've seen how we try to create a happy ending superficially (the castle in the air) or decisively dismiss any happy ending as artificial (the dungeon).

But once again, the invisible kingdom offers us a bifocal perspective. In-between a false, pious ending and a hopeless, defeated ending, the invisible kingdom reveals a battle taking place between good and evil.

Tolkien describes this state in-between: "No man can estimate what is really happening at the present. . . . All we do know, and that to a large extent by direct experience, is that evil labors with vast power and perpetual success—in vain: preparing always only the soil for unexpected good to sprout in."[2] Where have you seen good sprout from evil in your own life?

Write Your Heart Out

Take one story going on in your life right now, one situation that you worry about how it will turn out, and write the ending that you would like to see. Don't give way to the pious happily-ever-after ending and don't let your heart go to the dungeon, but write a realistic ending that you think would make sense. Pray that God will bring about your ending as it matches His.

For Tolkien and others who saw clearly into the invisible kingdom, no evil event, however horrible, was ever outside the story of salvation-history. God was and is constantly in the process of bending all events to his purposes. Such understanding doesn't make evil any less evil. As Tolkien put it in *The Silmarillion*, "Evil

NOTES

may yet be good to have been . . . and yet remain evil."[3] What do you think he meant by this? How can suffering and the death of our dreams propel us deeper into the invisible kingdom and toward greater dreams that satisfy?

Hundreds of years earlier, in the fourteenth century, God revealed this same truth to Julian of Norwich. A mystic and the first writer in English to be identified as a woman, the king entrusted this princess heart with a very powerful truth:

All shall be well

And all shall be well

And all manner of things shall be well.

Julian was the first to admit that she did not know how it would happen. She even confessed that she found it hard to believe, but she never once backed down from what the king had told her. And for centuries to follow, others have put their trust in the same promise. In the midst of the unexplainable, in the injustice of all that is unfair, in the sadness of everything that is left incomplete, there is peace in this hopeful, unassuming assurance. In the middle of the night, when despair tries to close in, when the diagnosis comes, when the husband leaves, when trouble arrives, or the money goes . . .

All shall be well.

Do you find yourself wanting to tell the Author how you think he should finish the story to your satisfaction? If you're like me, you want to place your order at the divine diner so you're assured of getting your suffering on the side. But we can't. What we can do is trust the King to do as he promised. Just as we have trusted him with our names and trusted him with our hearts, we can commit ourselves to trust him with the ending.

NOTES

What is the difference between being an optimist and believing that all will end well?

Why is optimism not enough to sustain us through suffering?

D OES THE SHOE FIT?

The rich and meaningful life we are looking for is possible, but it will not just happen. A string of days in succession on the calendar with too much to do will happen to us, but a life of meaning is something we have to pursue. Whatever ingredients are still in the fridge on a Friday night is what happens to us, but the meal we make from those ingredients is something we have to create. The things that shaped our hearts in the past have happened to us, but the kind of heart that comes from those things—a princess heart—is something we have to choose. Do you understand now how we choose a princess heart?

A KEY TO THE INVISIBLE KINGDOM

A princess translation of 2 Corinthians 4:16–18 might read this way:

Don't give up! I know it looks as though everything is falling apart on the outside. Look with the eyes of your heart at what is happening on the inside. The King is making a new way for you, grace upon grace. What you're going through right now seems crushing, but don't lose sight of what is coming. There is far more ahead than what meets the eye. What you see now will not even be here tomorrow, but what you can't see just yet will last forever.

NOTES

As we mature, we will face more and more of life, and we will also taste more and more of death. We will bury more loved ones, lose more dreams, and weather more storms. We will feel the inevitable incompleteness that is life on earth. But in the invisible kingdom, every death brings new life. The death of our little dreams calls us to find bigger ones: the kind of dreams that can't be stained or tainted or stolen by the world. As we lose or turn loose of some of those lesser dreams, we find we can replace them with dreams that are truly alive and are somehow older, as we are. We may think them less satisfying in the short run, but what they are lifting us toward will satisfy us forever.

Here's one example of what a princess heart in a not-so-fairy-tale world might look like:

In my mind's eye I can see a salt-and-pepper-haired stockbroker going into a meeting with a new awareness that she is a princess. None of her colleagues will notice a difference at first, but it won't take long. She stands a little taller and smiles much brighter, knowing that she is worth far more than the number of shares she sells. She gives her best in the presentation she makes, understanding for the first time in her life that the presentation doesn't make her. Her young, working-class dream was to grow wealthy and be surrounded with things of great value. Now her heart has found its own wealth and is dreaming of how to be of great value to the world. Now she has a name, Princess, and to her, that means everything.

> ### DIRECTIONS TO THE INVISIBLE KINGDOM
>
> *Now I saw a new heaven and a new earth, for the first heaven and the first earth had passed away. Also there was no more sea. Then I, John, saw the holy city, New Jerusalem, coming down out of heaven from God, prepared as a bride adorned for her husband. And I heard a loud voice from heaven saying, "Behold, the tabernacle of God is with men, and He will dwell with them, and they shall be His people. . . . And God will wipe away every tear from their eyes; there shall be no more death, nor sorrow, nor crying. There shall be no more pain, for the former things have passed away."*
>
> *Then He who sat on the throne said, "Behold, I make all things new." And He said to me, "Write, for these words are true and faithful."*
>
> *And He said to me, "It is done! I am the Alpha and the Omega, the Beginning and the End."*
>
> Revelation 21:1–6 NKJV

NOTES

Now write another example on your own:

In reading John's vision of the day of our dreams in Revelation 21:1–6, what do you find most hopeful and encouraging?

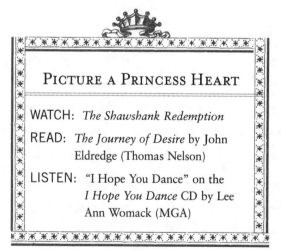

PICTURE A PRINCESS HEART

WATCH: *The Shawshank Redemption*

READ: *The Journey of Desire* by John Eldredge (Thomas Nelson)

LISTEN: "I Hope You Dance" on the *I Hope You Dance* CD by Lee Ann Womack (MGA)

The princesses will join the King. I can imagine us all gathering around, his ragtag band of daughters, called out and named by him, loved by the Prince, and secure in the ending. A single glass slipper here, a tarnished tiara there, a strand of pearls with just a few still intact. Stories to tell, grief to share, joys to celebrate.

NOTES

Some of us are walking, others limping, and some leaping. Though we are scarred and maimed from our trials and battles, though we are weary and wounded, we are more beautiful than ever, anticipating living out the grandest happily-ever-after of all time.

The Prayer of a Princess Heart

Father, your words are true and faithful. You will make all things new. We don't know how, but we can have a deep and abiding trust that you will. You are the Author of all history, and one day you will proclaim, "It is done. The Beginning has met the End." The inevitable will meet the unexpected, and our joy will be boundless. We will fall on our knees and worship you. We will finally understand what all of your promises mean. As we look back to the beginning from the end, we will see the meaning of the story you have written from the beginning of time. Until then, we will trust and cling to you as we walk along in the dark, illuminated by the light of your great love. Come, Lord Jesus. Fashion in us the true heart of a princess. In your name, amen.

•　•　•　•　•

NOTES

HOW WILL YOU TRUST YOUR HAPPILY EVER AFTER TO THE KING?
AND HOW WOULD YOU WANT THE WORLD TO LOOK
DIFFERENT BECAUSE OF YOUR PRINCESS HEART?

Write Your Heart Out

After completing this study, think about what you've discovered about your own princess heart and write a letter to yourself explaining how this study has changed you.

DEAR PRINCESS,

Love,

NOTES

Unless otherwise noted, quoted materials are from *Keeping a Princess Heart In a Not-So-Fairly-Tale World*, Nicole Johnson (Nashville: W Publishing Group, 2003).

PAGE XV

1. "Bridegroom," copyright © 2003, Christa Shore Ministries, LLC. Written and performed by Christa Shore and Beyond the Veil from their album *Beauty from Ashes*, produced by Morgan Cryar for Premier Records, Nashville, TN. All rights reserved. Used by permission. Purchase CD's or artwork online at www.christashore.org. The song "Bridegroom" from the CD *Beauty From Ashes* can be purchased online at www.christashore.org or www.princessheart.com.

CHAPTER 2

1. C. S. Lewis, *The Weight of Glory* (San Francisco: Harper San Francisco, 2000).

CHAPTER 3

1. Oswald Chambers, *My Utmost for His Highest* (Chicago: Moody Press, 1997).
2. C. S. Lewis, *The Weight of Glory* (San Francisco: Harper san Francisco, 2000).
3. Wayne Kirkpatrick, "Alice in Wonderland," *Angels of Mercy* by Susan Ashton (Capitol Records).

CHAPTER 4

1. C. S. Lewis, *The Four Loves* (New York: Harcourt Brace, 1991).

CHAPTER 6

1. George MacDonald, *The Princess and the Goblin* (New York: Dover Publications, 1999).
2. Augustine, *Confessions*. Public Domain.

CHAPTER 7

1. Daniel Boorstin, *The Image* (New York: Random House, 1961).

CHAPTER 8

1. J. R. R. Tolkien, *The Tolkien Reader* (New York: Ballantine Books, 1966).
2. Ibid.
3. J. R. R. Tolkien, *The Silmarillion.* (New York: Houghton Mifflin, 2001).

At a Glance

A Quick-Reference Guide

MOVIES TO WATCH

1. *Shrek*
2. *The Princess Diaries*
3. *Peggy Sue Got Married*
4. *The Hours* (Caution: This movie is Rated R. But the point it makes is significant.)
5. *The Magnificent Obsession*
6. *Roman Holiday*
7. *The Princess Bride*
8. *The Shawshank Redemption* (Caution: This movie is Rated R, but it makes a significant point.)

Add your favorite movies:

BOOKS TO READ

1. *Strong Women, Soft Hearts* by Paula Rinehart (W Publishing)
2. *Yearning* by Craig Barnes (InterVarsity Press)
3. *A Doll's House*, a play by Henrik Ibsen (Bantem Publishing)
4. *The Wounded Heart* by Dan Allender (NavPress)
5. *Rumors of Another World* by Philip Yancey (Zondervan)
6. *Forever, Erma: Best-Loved Writing from America's Favorite Humorist* by Erma Bombeck (MJF Books)
7. *The Sacred Romance* by John Eldredge and Brent Curtis (Thomas Nelson)
8. *The Journey of Desire* by John Eldredge (Thomas Nelson)

Add your favorite books:

_____

_____

_____

_____

_____

_____

_____

_____

_____

_____

_____

_____

_____

_____

_____

_____

MUSIC TO LISTEN TO

1. "Counting on a Miracle" on *The Rising* CD by Bruce Springsteen (Sony)
2. "Legacy" on the *Woven and Spun* CD by Nichole Nordeman (Sparrow)
3. "Alice in Wonderland" on the *Angels of Mercy* CD by Susan Ashton (Capitol)
4. "Isn't It Ironic?" on the *Jagged Little Pill* CD by Alanis Morissette (Maverick)
5. "That's What Faith Must Be" on *The Joy in the Journey* CD by Michael Card (Sparrow)
6. "This One's for the Girls" on the *Martina* CD by Martina McBride (RCA)
7. "Goodnight to a Mother's Dream" on the *Flyer* CD by Nanci Griffith
8. "I Hope You Dance" on the *I Hope You Dance* CD by Lee Ann Womack (MCA)

Add your favorite music:

_____

_____

_____

_____

_____

_____

_____

_____

_____

_____

_____

_____

_____

_____

_____

_____

_____

WHAT YOU'LL NEED FOR EACH LESSON

CHAPTER 1

IN PREPARATION

Read chapter 1, *Keeping a Princess Heart*.

Watch "Princess Heart" sketch, *Keeping a Princess Heart* DVD.

PICTURE A PRINCESS HEART

Watch: *Shrek*

Read: *Strong Women, Soft Hearts* by Paula Rinehart (W Publishing)

Listen: "Counting on a Miracle" on *The Rising* CD by Bruce Springsteen (Sony)

CHAPTER 2

IN PREPARATION

Read chapter 2, *Keeping a Princess Heart*.

Read a Brothers Grimm or Hans Christian Anderson fairy tale.

Read "Listen to Your Longings," *Fresh-Brewed Life* by Nicole Johnson (W Publishing).

PICTURE A PRINCESS HEART

Watch: *The Princess Diaries*

Read: *Yearning* by Craig Barnes (InterVarsity Press)

Listen: "Legacy" on the *Woven and Spun* CD by Nichole Nordeman (Sparrow)

SCRIPTURE

Psalm 38:9

Psalm 37:3–6

CHAPTER 3

IN PREPARATION

Read chapter 3, *Keeping a Princess Heart*.

PICTURE A PRINCESS HEART

Watch: *Peggy Sue Got Married*

Read: *A Doll's House*, a play by Henrik Ibsen

Listen: "Alice in Wonderland" on *Angels of Mercy* CD by Susan Ashton (Capitol)

SCRIPTURE

1 Corinthians 13

CHAPTER 4

IN PREPARATION

Read chapter 4, *Keeping a Princess Heart*.

Watch "Raising the Sail" sketch, *Keeping a Princess Heart* DVD.

PICTURE A PRINCESS HEART

Watch: *The Hours* [Warning: Rated R]

Read: *The Wounded Heart* by Dan Allender (NavPress)

Listen: "Isn't It Ironic?" on *Jagged Little Pill* CD by Alanis Morissette (Maverick)

SCRIPTURE

Luke 15: 11–32

CHAPTER 5

IN PREPARATION

Read chapter 5, *Keeping a Princess Heart*.

Watch "The Invisible Woman" sketch, *Keeping a Princess Heart* DVD.

PICTURE A PRINCESS HEART

Watch: *The Magnificent Obsession*

Read: *Rumors of Another World* by Philip Yancey (Zondervan)

Listen: "That's What Faith Must Be" on *The Joy in the Journey* CD by Michael Card (Sparrow)

SCRIPTURE

Romans 1:19–23

CHAPTER 6

IN PREPARATION

Read chapter 6, *Keeping a Princess Heart*.

Watch Walt Disney's *Snow White and the Seven Dwarfs*.

PICTURE A PRINCESS HEART

    Watch: *Roman Holiday*

    Read: *Forever, Erma: Best-Loved Writing from America's Favorite Humorist* by Erma Bombeck (MJF Books)

    Listen: "This One's for the Girls" on the *Martina* CD by Martina McBride (RCA)

SCRIPTURE

    Genesis 2:19

CHAPTER 7

IN PREPARATION

    Read chapter 7, *Keeping a Princess Heart.*

    Watch Walt Disney's *Cinderella.*

PICTURE A PRINCESS HEART

    Watch: *The Princess Bride*

    Read: *The Sacred Romance* by John Eldredge and Brent Curtis (Thomas Nelson)

    Listen: "Goodnight to a Mother's Dream" on the *Flyer* CD by Nanci Griffith

SCRIPTURE

    John 4:1–26

CHAPTER 8

IN PREPARATION

    Read chapter 8, *Keeping a Princess Heart.*

    Watch the Walt Disney's *Sleeping Beauty.*

PICTURE A PRINCESS HEART

    Watch: *The Shawshank Redemption* [Warning: Rated R]

    Read: *The Journey of Desire* by John Eldredge (Thomas Nelson)

    Listen: "I Hope You Dance" on the *I Hope You Dance* CD by Lee Ann Womack (MCA)

SCRIPTURE

    Revelation 21:1–6

The Faith, Hope, and Love Trilogy

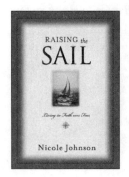

RAISING THE SAIL

Just as sailboats are made for the wind, women are made for relationships, and with both it takes faith to overcome the fear to let go and trust God's direction. Instead of frantically paddling or "motoring" our way through the seas of our emotional connections with each other, she challenges us to freely let go and trust the "Windmaker," God Himself, to help us find our way.

STEPPING INTO THE RING

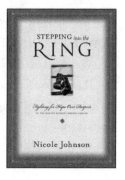

Where is the woman, old or young, who will not shed a tear but silently scream in her heart as she walks in these pages through the diagnosis of breast cancer and the devastation that ensues? While she focuses on the specific soul-chilling crisis, Nicole offers her readers broader insights for dealing with major losses of all kinds. She extends genuine hope and much-needed rays of light to those who are mired in hopelessness and despair.

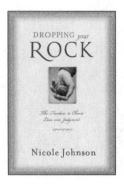

DROPPING YOUR ROCK

You can express your moral outrage by joining the angry mob howling for a sinner to be stoned. But what if that sinner is your friend, and you would rather change her heart than shed her blood? We don't have to hurl the rocks we clutch in our judgmental hands. With tender words and touching photos, Nicole Johnson guides us toward the "flat thud of grace" that can change our lives when we drop our rocks and choose to love instead.

W PUBLISHING GROUP
A Division of Thomas Nelson Publishers
Since 1798

How Can a Woman Live with Hope . . . In the Midst of Reality?

WOMEN OF FAITH

KEEPING A PRINCESS HEART

Every little girl grew up hearing the stories of "happily ever after," but finds it hard to believe that such a world still exists today. *Keeping a Princess Heart* is a deeply thoughtful exploration of the tension women feel between what they *long for* and what they *live with*. Women will discover how to hold on to their dreams as they take a deep, trusting dive into the wonderful world of fairy tales to reclaim a hidden treasure: a princess heart.

W PUBLISHING GROUP
A Division of Thomas Nelson Publishers
Since 1798

INSPIRE YOUR
Princess Heart

. . . with this visual companion available on DVD or VHS. These dramatic presentations illustrate the chapters in Nicole's book and in this guide and personalize each of the lessons. The blending of Nicole's unique gift of writing and theatre will illuminate what you're gaining from this workbook as you discover your Princess Heart.

★ ★ ★

These products are only available at Nicole's website. To place an order of *Keeping a Princess Heart* in DVD or VHS visit PrincessHeart.com